HOUSES *that* SUGAR BUILT

An Intimate Portrait of Philippine Ancestral Homes

ORO
EDITIONS

"Novato, CA"

CONTENTS

Introduction

Memoir

The Houses

❀ ILOILO ❀

❀ NEGROS OCCIDENTAL ❀

❀ PAMPANGA ❀

Essay

Glossary

Acknowledgements

Contributors

The houses we live in leave some of the most lasting impressions on us: the atmosphere of our family life, the issues we take on throughout our lifetime. Behind these old walls that separated us from the world outside, the family grew up, and we lived through joys and sorrows as the years went by so unrelentingly.

Brazilian Modernist Oscar Niemeyer, in *The Curves of Time*, translated from the Portuguese by Izabel Murat Burbridge, London: Phaidon Press, 2000, p. 7

Critical Ambition:

THE PHILIPPINE "BIG HOUSE"

Until thirty years ago the Philippines could offer many well-preserved examples of Spanish architecture of the sixteenth and seventeenth centuries. Intramuros, the old walled stronghold of Manila … which was once a treasure-house of ultramarine Hispanic art, suffered irreparable damage in the Second World War.
- Sir Banister Fletcher's *A History of Architecture,* London: The Athlone Press, 1975, p. 1114

If the Philippines has figured in historical architectural accounts, it has chiefly been as a footnote to Spanish or American architectural traditions – or a fleeting mention such as that above from Sir Banister Fletcher's magisterial *History of Architecture*. Such passing references do scant justice to the rich architectural legacy to be found across the archipelago – particularly in the houses of Iloilo, Negros Occidental and Pampanga, its main sugar-producing provinces.

These "houses that sugar built" have been described in local publications. However, they have yet to receive the international exposure achieved by equally distinctive groups of residences outside the Western architectural canon – possibly because their poise and assurance places them somewhat outside the field occupied by their contemporaries and near-contemporaries elsewhere. Although financed from the profits of a lucrative primary industry, they are not as outlandish as the extravagant palaces of early 20th-century Baku's Caspian "oil barons"; nor are they as obsessively varied as the nationalist confections of Cairo's 1920s Garden City. And although mostly situated well into the 20th century, they are not as achingly modern as the villas of the El Pedregal estate, Mexico's showcase for "starchitects" like Luis Barragán.

Nonetheless, they are important in two crucial ways. Firstly, although swiftly classified in terms of architectural style – and virtually every owner spoken to is eager to learn which category their house falls into – upon experiencing the buildings themselves there are almost always layers of additional influence. An Art Deco villa may exhibit strong traces of Purism or Bauhaus-derived tendencies in its massing. A conventional Neoclassical mansion might, upon venturing inside, reveal a world of Mannerist extravagance.

The second aspect is that this assured blending of styles reveals what we might call a Critical Ambition – a desire on the part of their patrons to participate in an international architectural culture. Their relatively overlooked location did not stop the sugar barons responsible for these houses from undertaking a 20th-century form of the Grand Tour of Western capitals, returning with a craving to bring the latest trends from Paris or Vienna to the provincial Philippines, or to partake of the latest streamlined "Moderne" style from the USA. In our complacently globalised world, it is important to remember the scale and ambition that would have underpinned this cultural commitment in the early 20th century.

As Gina Consing McAdam's description here highlights, the Villanueva family of Bacolod referred to their home – listed here as the Generoso M Villanueva Mansion – as "Daku Balay" ("Big House" in Ilonggo). Ireland-born photographer Siobhán Doran was intrigued to note that this term shares its Iberian directness with the Anglo-Irish name for such residences – the "Big House". (The English, by contrast, tend towards the more verbose "country seat" or "stately home".) Valerie Pakenham, herself custodian of a "family castle" in the Irish Midlands, recalls, in her 2000 book *The Big House in Ireland*, one definition of owning such a residence as "something between a predicament and a *raison d'être*". Siobhán's photographs in this volume aim to show off the Philippine houses in all their variety. Her architectural background makes her ideally suited to get "beneath the skin" of these unique residences.

Owing to her family history and intimate connections with many of these mansions, Gina is able to highlight some key points in their family histories and to enrich the house profiles with anecdotes shared by owners and heirs. Her memoir aims to set the dwellings within their social and historical context, and her individual house descriptions transport us back to a time when these residences were in their elegant heyday. Nonetheless, it is evident that they were essentially family homes – domestic havens from the outside world.

Ian McDonald's overview aims to place the "houses that sugar built" alongside other examples within a broad architectural spectrum. It investigates three main areas that confront similar non-Western structures: the "commodity-house" aspect of these residences (their grounding in a profitable trade in a commodity), their possible role in the search for a national style and their relationship with the local vernacular. In doing so, Ian hopes to pay tribute to the critical ambition demonstrated by these extraordinary houses.

"WHERE IS THIS HOUSE?"
"ARE THERE ANY MORE LIKE IT?"

A Memoir by Gina Consing McAdam

It was after dinner at my home in London five years ago, in 2018, when Siobhán asked the first question and Ian the next. They'd both spotted the black-and-white image of an ornately styled, unusually large house in the small alcove at the top of the stairs. The picture showed my family's ancestral home in the Philippines. Yes, there were many more like it, built around the same time, in the 1920s and 1930s, when sugar from Iloilo, Negros Occidental and Pampanga – three of the Philippines' main sugar-producing provinces – was in peak demand.

I grew up in a house that sugar built. Not in any of the aforementioned places but in urban Manila, where my grandfather – a doctor, politician and sugar planter from Molo in Iloilo City (the capital of Iloilo Province on the island of Panay) – put up a house for his family. My father and his brothers were studying then at the Ateneo de Manila, the Jesuit-run institution meant to turn callow boys into thinking men; their only sister had graduated from the Assumption Iloilo, an all-girls convent school. My grandmother had been part of its first intake, when it started as a boarding school in 1910.

Our Manila house was built much later than the family home in Iloilo, 280 miles away, but its interiors are not dissimilar. The sweeping processional staircase set against a concrete wall, the monogrammed doors with panels of French-embossed glass and the green terrazzo floors trimmed with red geometric lines – all echo the spirit of our ancestral house in Molo, which in 2014 was bought and beautifully restored by a major real-estate group.

When an architect friend in the Philippines learned that Siobhán, Ian and I had decided to work together on a book on houses built by *hacienderos*, or sugar planters, he generously sent me an article entitled "Iloilo Builds and Builds". It had been featured in a 1939 issue of the *Sunday Tribune* magazine, a weekly periodical published in Manila from 1925 to 1945. In it, the author, Catalino G Garingalao Jr, described a slice of Iloilo City's flourishing domestic architecture:

The city of Manila no longer enjoys the sole and distinctive reputation of being the seat of many fine residences built and designed by prominent civil engineers and architects … Iloilo is going [through] a house-beautiful-building boom. In fact, it has been going on for some time. Which also shows that Iloilo has not been much affected by the depression.

Nationally known as the beehive of sugar barons and captains of commerce and industry, Iloilo has been made richer by the distribution of the sugar processing tax[1] among its sugar planters who have used part of the money to build mansions all over the province.

Whether or not it was indeed a windfall from the sugar tax that helped to fund the construction of their residences, Iloilo's urban vista was now enlivened by the porticos and parapets of planters' houses – particularly in and around Molo and Jaro, its two most prosperous enclaves.

Among the "outstanding modern houses" singled out in the *Sunday Tribune* piece were a number featured in this book, including the "ultra-modern" mansion of Eugenio Lopez (the Lopez Boat House), "the co-owner of the many transportation concerns … besides owning a number of sugar centrals [mills] and haciendas", and the house of the former Governor of Iloilo that "with its arches and colonnades … looks like a capitol building" (the Yusay-Consing Ancestral House). Whereas these houses may have seemed remarkable for their modernity and, to an extent, ostentation, today they are considered reflective of the

A plethora of excellent articles and books by historians and academics will offer a far richer study of the complex history of sugar in the Philippines, once this Southeast Asian country's paramount export commodity. But hopefully, what follows will help to at least provide some context.

The 1890s to the 1930s were the apogee of the Philippine sugar industry. Towards the end of more than three centuries of Spanish rule – the Spanish colonial era in the Philippines lasted from 1565 to 1898 – sugar was the crop that minted fortunes. Pampanga's sugar planters benefited from the province's proximity to Manila, where the Spaniards had opened the port to international trade in 1834. By 1857, sugar from Pampanga was being processed in a refinery located in Malabon.

Further south, in the group of islands known as the Visayas, the Spaniards would open the Port of Iloilo to world markets in 1855. The following year, a young English businessman, Nicholas Loney, would return to the Philippines as Britain's vice consul. The demand for sugar in Western markets was high; European trading houses such as Ker & Co and Ynchausti & Company, with stations along Iloilo's waterfront, were flourishing, and Loney was tasked with finding ways to help increase the Philippines' sugar-producing capacity. He would learn that the soil on nearby Negros Island, still very much virgin territory, was particularly conducive to growing sugarcane.

What followed was mass migration to Negros among many of Iloilo's well-to-do families, eager to expand their fortunes by acquiring vast tracts of land cheaply, which they then turned into *haciendas*. Loney is said to have encouraged sugar production by offering loans, introducing new technologies and providing expertise honed during the Industrial Revolution in Europe. Iloilo's sugar farms, in terms of hectarage, were smaller than the sprawling Negros plantations. However, Iloilo remained the "mother ship" and, in many cases, migrants – including several of my father's uncles (it was nearly all men who *initially* set forth) – decided to farm and settle their immediate families in Negros.

The demand for Philippine sugar rose even further during the Spanish–American War in 1898, when the US ceased buying sugar from Cuba. This was also the year when a group of Ilonggo[2] sugar planters led by Aniceto Lacson (cousin of Juan Anson Lacson, whose house is featured here) and Juan Araneta led an uprising against the Spanish

accomplishments of local sons and daughters.

My siblings and I, and our first cousins, were all raised in Manila. We knew that the family business was primarily sugar, based on the islands of Panay and Negros in the region of the Philippines called the Visayas. But our fathers had been encouraged to pursue lucrative professions, so the state of the industry and the family fortunes tied to it were hardly mentioned. The whole *hacienda* thing was like a precious piece of heirloom jewellery, quietly hidden, retrieved and worn only on rare occasions such as our joyful clan gatherings ("family reunions") in Bacolod, the capital of Negros Occidental, or else when we were reminded of it by my father's eldest brother, who either by reasons of default or ascendancy ran the entire show.

Then, of course, there were the consecutive summers spent visiting farms and fishponds in Negros and Iloilo, where we slept under mosquito nets, hunted for ghosts and played hide and seek, indifferent to the constant clacking of the mahjong tiles of our elders: our summer soundtrack, as predictable as our fathers' visits from Manila every two weeks.

The annual, month-long spells in our *hacienda* in Capiz, then a largely rural province adjacent to Iloilo, were half boot camp, half Alice in Wonderland. My father's youngest brother built a single-storey house in the middle of cane fields partly inspired by the Japanese *minka* – complete with sliding panel doors, or *shoji*. To reach it, we even had to cross a slightly arched bridge, but it had no electricity or running water. It did seem a reprieve to be brought back to the cities where, before returning to Manila, we dutifully paid homage to our elderly relatives in their houses with many rooms. As to our making a living off the land, the reality was not so simple. By the 1970s and 1980s, when we were coming of age, sugar was no longer the magic money tree of the late 19th and early 20th centuries.

colonisers in Negros, a victory that led to the short-lived Negros Cantonal Government.

After Spain ceded the Philippines to the Americans in 1898, there was much to favour the planting of sugarcane – including the time of relative stability that was the American colonial period. That era begat the Philippine Commonwealth Government in 1935, and, at its end, the establishment of the Republic of the Philippines in 1946. During this time, a cascade of treaties saw Philippine sugar exempted from US export tariffs and subject to favourable quotas. Several sugar planters, or professionals with planting roots, would enter regional and national politics; many were merely following in the path of their forefathers, who had held important municipal positions as part of the Filipino *ilustrado* (educated, wealthy intelligentsia) class during the Spanish era. One prominent and influential sugar planter, Eugenio Jalandoni Lopez – grandfather of namesake Eugenio and his brother Fernando Lopez (whose homes are featured here) – showed his reforming zeal even before the conclusion of the Spanish era, when, as Mayor of Jaro in the 1870s, he called for an end to labour practices such as debt peonage that, under Spanish rule, had undermined human dignity.

The sugar industry was all but decimated during the Second World War, when the Japanese occupied the Philippines between 1941 and 1945 – disrupting, if not ruining, lives and livelihoods, and necessitating the revival of the industry after the war (or "liberation", as several of the older members of sugar-planter families still refer to the end of the Japanese occupation).

The experience of living through the war is still very much seared into the minds of a number of the more elderly house owners, custodians or relatives that I consulted while writing this book; all were children at the time, and all were eager to share their direct experiences or those of their parents. For the current generation of owners and custodians, these "war stories" are now part of cherished family lore.

Luci Lizares Yunque, who also describes how her aunts used to change dresses as often as three times during parties, said that she was told how her grandparents strove to retain the family's high standards – even as they escaped on a boat from Talisay in Negros taking their entire household and the family's grand piano, which provided some entertainment at sea as a butler served dinner in white gloves.

Asuncion "Nena" Jalandoni Yaptangco, 93, says that her older brother Venecio, at the time a member of the Reserve Officers Training Corps (ROTC), was recruited to fight the Japanese and survived the infamous Death March of Filipino and American prisoners of war ("Everyone wanted to fight for the Philippines. My mother was always praying"). Luis Yusay Consing, 87, recalls how his brother Arturo cheated death when he missed the last sailing of the ill-fated SS *Corregidor* from Manila in December 1941; the ship hit a landmine and sank. Carmela Javellana Ledesma, 87, told me that as children, while escaping the carpet bombing of Luzon, they had to walk down the mountains of Baguio, the Philippines' summer capital, where many planter families had sought refuge from the Japanese. Her mother instructed her older children to roll food tins inside their blankets, while she kept the family's cash underneath canisters of "Klim" – infant formula milk – for her two babies.

After the Second World War, in addition to compensation from the Japanese and Americans, the 1955 Laurel–Langley Agreement between the US and the Philippines led to the industry's renaissance: there would be no quotas on the amount of sugar that could be exported to the United States, and Americans could invest freely in Philippine industries. Once again, the industry flourished.

But by the 1970s, the agreement had expired, world demand for sugar plunged and the situation was compounded by the creation of a sugar monopoly. Thereafter, the industry underwent a steep decline and with it the fortunes of sugar planters and, equally important, the livelihoods and well-being of sugar workers. Some enlightened members of the old planter families were quick to pivot to alternative occupations, such as the cooperative led by my aunt Dolores Locsin Consing to support the retraining of farm workers in the production of handicrafts using native materials – thus helping give birth to Negros' successful handicrafts industry.

Land reform, the seeds of which had been sown as far back as the 1950s, culminated in the 1980s with the implementation of the Comprehensive Agrarian Reform Program (CARP). Agricultural lands were divided and redistributed to landless farmers and farm workers across the Philippines. Thus, for many sugar planters and their families, the old certainties – including the cocoon of

Governor Consing (in black tuxedo) hosts a formal dinner for members of the clergy at what is now known as the Yusay-Consing Ancestral House (Molo Mansion), October 1932

paternalism and feudalism that went with them – have all but vanished. Or have they?

In 2023, several old planter families who have retained their stake in sugar are once again finding their feet – falling back on the entrepreneurial spirit of their forefathers and creating new sources of income and revenue. Many continue to farm, while combining farming with other businesses. Several sugar mills and refineries in Iloilo and Negros are now owned by conglomerates run by second- and third-generation members of entrepreneurial families whose interests, in Manila and elsewhere in the Philippines, go far beyond sugar. Yet they have chosen to invest in the industry with a clear eye to the future.

My co-author, Siobhán Doran, and I are delighted to have been given access to photograph these houses and speak to their owners and custodians. While the world has evolved around them, they remain a particularly resilient tribe. The Gaston family (Gaston Ancestral House) can trace their roots back to a Frenchman, but many are from the influential and "economically dominant" Chinese mestizo community, who built Molo and Jaro during the Spanish era. Before the lure of sugar on Negros Island, they were at the centre of the weaving industry and the professions. Many families inter-married through the generations, strengthening both social and economic ties.

It is evident that almost every family that enjoyed the 40–50 boom years of the sugar industry – whether they came from Iloilo, Negros Occidental or Pampanga – shared the same life experiences and values.

Besides the adversity of the Second World War, there was the deep reverence for religion, with the ritualistic recital of the daily rosary and the Angelus at 6pm. There was the investment in the finest educations money could buy – in Manila, but also in the United States and Europe. The cultivation, especially among the girls but also among the boys, of music, art, literature and dance was expected – with the exceptionally talented being sent to New York, to schools like Mannes and Juilliard, and again to Europe. The lust for travel – considered a necessary indulgence – included "Grand Tours" lasting months on end, with

some families leasing apartments for the duration in Madrid, Paris or New York. The respect for "ascendancy" or age-related "hierarchies" within the family was so well demonstrated by the seating arrangements at the dining table, where the father sits at the head, the mother to his right and the eldest child to his left. The "simple" daily lifestyle, devoid of artifice, contrasted with the grand manner in which they entertained at home, where families could show off their exquisite Japanese and European tableware and other rare collections as well as the talent of their children, who played musical instruments, performed plays, danced or recited poetry for their guests.

For Ilonggos, there was also the participation in such traditions as the "Kahirup Ball", which, while held in Manila, drew together members of mainly sugar-planter families in a splendid evening of dancing and fashion showmanship.

It is not lost on me that my family's ancestral house is the only one in this book that is no longer in family hands.

The biographer Hermione Lee said that "the loss of the childhood family home ... is bound with a feeling of alienation ... as the remembered place now belongs to someone else, and is going in time, to be the site of *their* nostalgic memory, *their* sense of loss".[3] My family, including first and second cousins, is extremely fortunate, and proud, that the house we sold has been so well preserved and maintained by its generous new owners, with their keen sense of heritage and destiny. They have made sure that the house has retained its place as a 1920s architectural icon and a powerful symbol of sugar's glory days, with the foundations laid by our great-grandparents still intact.

Yet, another family, one that has been assiduous in holding on, in whatever form, to its ancestral pile, a magnificent monument to what sugar built, must surely draw pleasure from knowing that it is still theirs – their own remembered place.

Notes

[1] The sugar tax was imposed by the US Government on sugar refineries in the United States. Sugar planters in the Philippines were compensated by the US Government for sugarcane that had to be destroyed in 1934–35 owing to the temporary curtailment of quotas on the import of sugar – quotas that had been favourable to planters.
[2] People from Iloilo and Negros Occidental; the term also refers to the language, Hiligaynon.
[3] Hermione Lee, "A House of Air", in K Kennedy and H Lee (eds), *Lives of Houses,* Princeton, NJ: Princeton University Press, 2020, p. 32.

All images in this essay courtesy of Gina Consing McAdam

Apart from the obvious fact of their being interesting architectural subjects, the houses featured in this book were chosen on the basis of two things: *kinship* and *friendship.* Kinship because their owners were either directly or indirectly related to my family, or else they were close and trusted friends of people without whom this book would not have happened.

Gina Consing McAdam

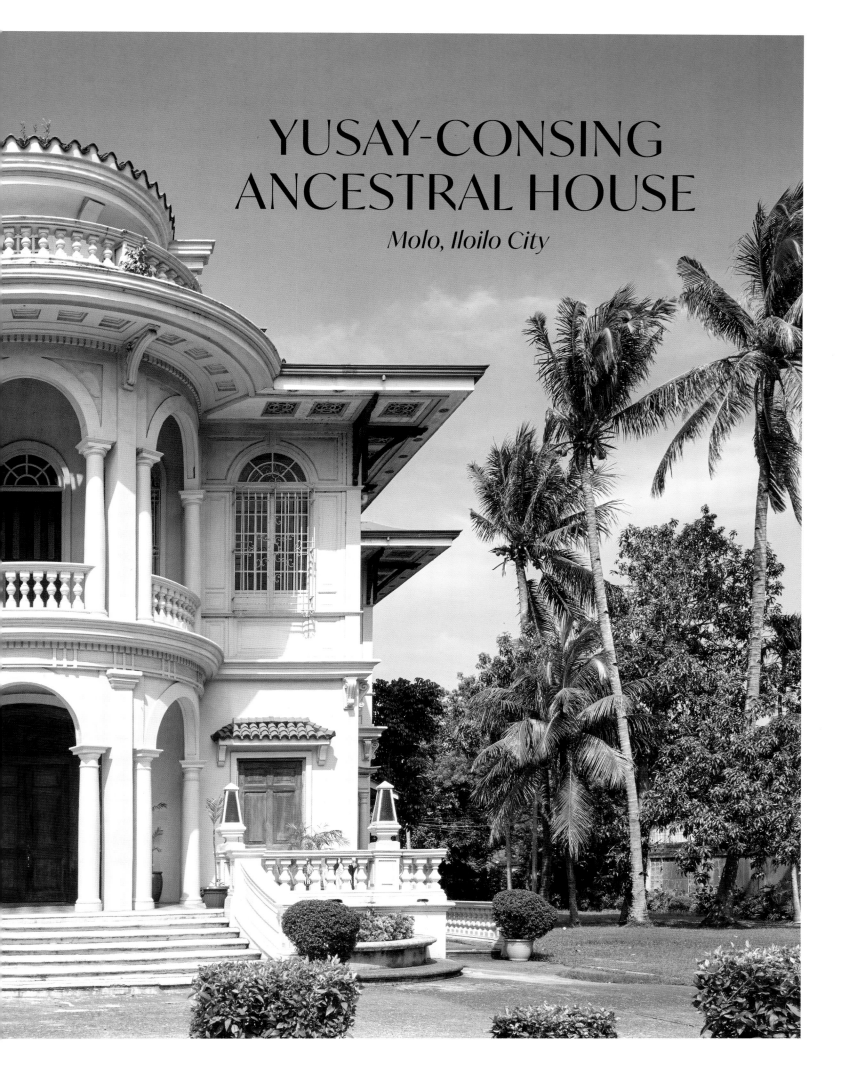

YUSAY-CONSING ANCESTRAL HOUSE

Molo, Iloilo City

Justice and Politics

With its spectacular Neoclassical façade, flirtatious lines and Art Deco flourishes, the Yusay-Consing Ancestral House is a sight to behold.

Perched prominently on the newly restored Molo Plaza directly in front of the Neo-Gothic Santa Ana church, it is a vision that says everything there is to know about the heyday of the sugar industry.

When the family sold the house to a large Philippine business conglomerate in 2014, inhabitants of Molo, Iloilo feared the worst. Would the new owners demolish one of the great symbols of Iloilo's belle époque?

Reassuringly, SM Prime decided to make the house a shining example of adaptive reuse. Its restoration and revival as the "Molo Mansion" – a thriving retail enterprise, cultural hub and event space – has returned the house to its former grandeur. In its present incarnation, the house continues to attract favourable publicity for the Ilonggo people and culture.

But had they still been living there, the original owners would surely have baulked at the exposure. They were notoriously private people, leading one of their contemporaries to say, "This family never opened the gates to their house. They seemed to be from another world."

Luis Yusay Consing, 87, known as "Louie" or "Baby", is the youngest and only surviving son of Rosario "Ayong" Yusay Consing, the daughter of Petra Lacson Yusay who commissioned the residence in 1926 in honour of her late husband, Estanislao. She built the house as it stands today with the assistance of Rosario's husband, Dr Timoteo "Tiong" Yusay Consing Sr, said to have been her favourite son-in-law.

The family's reputation for privacy can be traced to its matriarch, whom they called "Lola Pe [Grandmother Pe]". As she grew more elderly, she was often in poor health and prone to staying indoors:

Lola Pe was a quiet, old lady. Her being sickly was also the reason why Papa [Timoteo] came to live in the house. For him, it was a sacrifice as he had worked very hard to build a chalet near the Iloilo River for Mama. But Lola Pe wanted him to come and live with her. He was a doctor and she trusted him.
- Luis Yusay Consing, *grandson of Petra Lacson Yusay*

In the last few years, the mansion's architect has been confirmed as Paris-born Andrés Luna de San Pedro, son of the Filipino artist Juan Luna (whose *The Battle of Lepanto*, painted in 1887, hangs in the Palacio de Senado in Madrid). Luis recalls being told by his mother that Timoteo Sr, already a popular young physician, supervised the construction of the house on Petra's behalf. The interior, while austere, would be stylishly appointed with Art Deco furniture by the House of Puyat, once the Philippines' most coveted furniture makers, and ornaments collected during the family's many European travels.

While Petra was alive, the house was the epicentre of the Yusay clan – even as most of the sons and daughters married and moved away, either to Manila, the capital of the Philippines, or, in the case of the sons, to Negros Occidental.

The late, great Philippine architect and heritage-conservation expert Augusto F Villalón tagged the Yusay-Consing Mansion as *hacienda*-style, a type that was widespread in the country under the Americans – and, as we shall see, the house also harbours important connections with the Philippine Commonwealth era. The imposing façade, its broad central entrance topped with a roofed balcony overlooking a neat garden, speaks of the plantation-based affluence of Ilonggos involved in the sugar trade.

The house boasts locally made tiles, hardwood panels and handcrafted elements. However, not all is "archetypal": in this otherwise classic residence, the dining room and kitchen were on the upper floor along with some of the bedrooms. Equally uncommon, the room above the car porch was once a small library.

Throughout, broad circulation spaces facilitate airflow and the lofty ground-floor ceiling likewise contributes to all-important ventilation in this tropical climate. Today, its height accommodates a jaw-dropping chandelier of cascading *capiz* shells, the centrepiece of the former *sala* (living room). Here, the ribbed, original ceiling is punctuated by floral timber bosses, while the fielded, panelled balustrades of the hardwood staircase sweep outwards at the base.

According to research by historian Roque Hofileña Jr, Estanislao Yusay was "one of the most brilliant lawyers of Iloilo and Negros", serving as the chief legal counsel of Aniceto Lacson – who, together with Juan Araneta, led the famous 1898 Negros uprising against the Spaniards.

Estanislao died in 1911, having reached the position of Manila's Judge of the Court of First Instance.

Petra and Estanislao had 10 children: Jose, Ramon, Enrique, Vicenta, Rosario, Trinidad, Mariano, Manuela, Soledad and Manuel. The family took pride in sending three sons to the finest schools: Yale (Jose), Harvard (Ramon) and the University of Paris (Enrique). In Manila, they had a house on Calle San Luis in Ermita – then the capital's premier residential district, its layout indebted to US architect Daniel Burnham's turn-of-the-century "City Beautiful" movement (also an influence on the Burnham-designed Philippine summer capital of Baguio). Luis remembers his Mama telling him that when she was a young girl, they heard José Rizal, the Philippine national hero, being executed for sedition in nearby Bagumbayan (now Luneta Park). As the firing-squad shots rang out, Petra shouted "Han matado a Rizal!" ("They've killed Rizal!") and ordered her children to fall on their knees and pray.

Timoteo Sr and Rosario's six children – Timoteo Jr (known as "Nene"), Mario, Anita, Arturo, Horacio and Luis – were raised in the house almost entirely before and

The design was typical in the Visayas – *bordado* [a reference to embroidery],
coquettish with all its lacework on the outside

Augusto F Villalón, quoted in Marge C Enriquez, "The Molo Mansion gets a Makeover", *Cocoon*, Vol. 9, Issue 2 (2016), p. 79

We didn't think of ourselves as living in such a big house. It was simply a home to us. As children, we played inside the house but more usually on the grounds because the grounds measured about a hectare. My father planted mango trees. I used to climb the trees to pick ripe mangoes and eat them while hanging above the street.

Luis Yusay Consing

after the Second World War. When Petra died in 1948, their parents took it over. Nene once told his young nieces how, while standing on the front balcony, he watched the night sky over Molo turn orange as the houses of their relatives and friends went up in flames – torched by either Filipino guerrillas or the American defenders.

It was Horacio who as a young boy was Petra's chosen favourite; he would sleep in her bedroom with his nurse. Every day at the same hour, Horacio would stand by her window facing Molo Plaza for a glimpse of his uncle Pedro Ditching's burgundy Hudson Terraplane – a rare sight on the streets of Iloilo – driving past.

According to Luis, the public life of the house was almost entirely owing to his Papa rather than the shy Yusays. One aunt, Manuela, was the exception; beautiful and coquettish, she was closely involved in the Kahirup Club, a social organisation set up and run by members of Ilonggo sugar-planter families.

Timoteo Sr was appointed to the governorship of Iloilo twice: the last to serve under an American governor general and the first under the Philippine Commonwealth Government. During his period of office in the 1930s, he would host leaders of the Catholic Church and national politicians in the mansion, including President Manuel L Quezon and Vice President Sergio Osmeña – in grand Ilonggo style.

By the 1960s, Timoteo and Rosario began to spend increasingly more time in Manila. It was their eldest son, Nene, then the President of Passi Sugar Central, who would carry on his parents' and grandparents' legacies of family stewardship. With their ancestral house still standing, the descendants of Estanislao and Petra Yusay, and Timoteo and Rosario Consing, can continue to draw inspiration from this monument to their achievements.

CASA MARIQUIT

Jaro, Iloilo City

An Imperishable World

Until the house came to be known by Salvacion "Mariquit" Javellana Lopez's sobriquet, she would often refer to her childhood home as the Santa Isabel house, after the Jaro street on which it stands.

When her husband, Fernando "Nanding" Hofileña Lopez, a former Vice President of the Philippines, passed away in 1993 and their eldest grandson asked her where she wanted to live, she said, "In Santa Isabel."

Perhaps this was a reference to the area surrounding Jaro Cathedral five minutes away; after all, Santa Isabel is the Spanish variation of St Elizabeth, the cathedral's patron saint from Hungary. It may seem strange that 13th-century Spain should have a connection to a Hungarian saint, but

King James I of Aragon was married to a princess of the Hungarian House of Árpád: Violant – or, in Spanish, *Yolanda de Hungría* – providing another example of the Philippines' unusually varied cultural connections with the wider world.

On hearing his grandmother's preference, Robert "Panchito" Lopez Puckett replied, "If so, we will have to fix it up first." The same restoration team that had worked on the walled city of Intramuros in Manila was commissioned to

This house occupies a special place in Iloilo history. I appreciate it even more now
because I see that others do. You don't get houses like this anymore.

Risa Maria Lourdes O. Peña Sarabia, *great-granddaughter of Salvacion "Mariquit" Javellana Lopez*

undertake the project. "It took a full year with 20 labourers," recalls Panchito. "They chipped the white paint off the external brickwork, and the paint from the walls inside. Twenty coats of paint had been added through the years by various tenants. My grandmother hadn't lived in that house since she eloped with my grandfather in 1924."

The original mahogany floors were stripped of accumulated wax and the painted internal walls replaced with wood panelling. The roof was likewise changed. "After everything she'd spent on the work, and the fact that she gave it to us, we decided to call it Casa Mariquit." Today, Panchito and his half-brother Rito "Judgee" Lopez Peña are co-owners of this fine example of a *bahay na bato* ("house of stone") structure built during Spanish colonial rule. It is possibly one of the most accessible of Iloilo's ancestral homes still owned by the original family. Visitors are often toured around by the caretaker, who lives on the grounds.

Casa Mariquit is said to have been constructed in 1803 (making it by far the oldest of the houses in this book). It

was owned by Mariquit's grandfather, Julio Quiambong Javellana, a half-Chinese, half-Filipino banker. "They kept the money safely hidden under the hardwood floors of the anteroom and master's bedroom. At the time, banks were not stand-alone buildings but were located in homes. But in 1910 or 1911, they built a big safe on the ground floor," Panchito explains. The house would pass to Julio's son, Ramon Javellana, who married Leonor Virto. Their only

daughter, Mariquit, was just three years old when her father died, and his young widow would go on to marry his cousin Vicente Javellana. Mariquit inherited the house, part of her considerable Javellana fortune.

The ground floor of the two-storey Casa Mariquit is made of exposed brick. To arrive at the double entrance doors, one passes a trio of *barrigon* windows (the name given to windows with bulging, "pot-bellied" grilles) and an ancient

banyan tree (known as *balete* in the Philippines). What must have been a large *silong* (open ground floor) is now a relatively confined space. This is probably because at one time the ground floor was remodelled to form the living quarters of Panchito and Judgee's mother, Yolanda "Bobbie" Lopez; Judgee; his wife, Sarah; and their young family.

A key part of Casa Mariquit's story is that Bobbie was the headstrong, vivacious eldest daughter of Mariquit and

Nanding. On 1 April 1946, she married James Robert Puckett, a dashing US Army officer and member of General Douglas MacArthur's forces sent to liberate the Philippines from the Japanese. At her 21st birthday party, he'd introduced himself with the words "Come on, Bobbie, let's dance." In time, they divorced, and she would marry again. In her later years, she entertained frequently in Casa Mariquit, moving up to the first floor, until she went to live with Judgee in his new home in La Paz a few miles away.

From the ground floor, a single-flight, ornamental staircase culminates in an anteroom that until recently housed a display honouring Vice President Lopez, who was also the first Mayor of Iloilo City, a Philippine senator and a principal in the business foreshadowing Lopez Holdings Corporation, today one of the Philippines' largest conglomerates. With an eye to posterity, Panchito has donated to the National Museum of the Philippines

numerous artefacts including his grandfather's desk and a life-size portrait by National Artist Fernando Amorsolo.

What remains constitutes a substantial legacy. The many louvred doors are made of yakal wood, and the interiors' dominant palette leans towards dark yew. With his wife, Dr Ruby Miranda Puckett, Panchito has managed to populate its spaces – including the small prayer room (*oratorio*) off the dining room – with choice antique furnishings, where they no longer boasted their original fittings, in order to suggest the lifestyle of their former occupants. The *sala mayor* (main living room) with its commanding double doors and ornate fretwork leads to other rooms, mini-repositories of dreams and lives past.

According to Panchito, Mariquit did go back to live for a while in her family home before she died. This may not be the largest house that sugar built, but the exquisite Casa Mariquit is equally emblematic of what was once thought an imperishable world.

I asked my grandfather, who is renting the upper portion of the house? Because when I went to visit my mother, they were stomping their feet and it seemed like the house was about to fall down. He told me who they were and that they paid a rent of 1,000 pesos. I asked him if he would let me rent it for 3,000 pesos. My grandmother slapped the table with the palm of her hand and said I could have it for free.

Robert "Panchito" Puckett, *grandson of Salvacion "Mariquit" Javellana Lopez*

ARGUELLES-JALANDONI HOUSE

Jaro, Iloilo City

Steeped
in Prayer

Standing amid the bustle of Graciano Lopez
Jaena Park in Jaro is a house that proudly
projects its heart.

Among the many treasured mementos displayed in
the Arguelles-Jalandoni mansion is an "oil photo"
that hangs in a simple frame, dated 1949. It depicts
the house as it looked just after it was built in 1927. The
robust façade is chamfered at the street corner, its main
balcony positioned at an angle clearly visible to the prelates
of Jaro Cathedral diagonally opposite. Lancet arches run
the length of the upper storey, framing coloured fanlights
and emerald-patterned balcony doors. On the ground
floor underneath, an arcade shields a series of Gothic-style
"cathedral" doors. And parked alongside the arches is a
slick, black, imported Model T Ford – a luxury for its time.

This is one house in which the architecture visibly
captures the essence of its original owner, Agatona
Arguelles-Jalandoni. Built in 1927 with Agatona's name
inscribed above the ornate corner parapet, the mansion's
windows and doors would not have looked out of place in

My father, who was an orphan, was the adopted son of my grandmother, whom he loved very much. She was actually his aunt. During the Second World War, when they had to flee Jaro, Daddy rode on the *carroza* with his mother, who could not do the walk.

Regina "Jean" Jalandoni, *owner and house custodian*

a chapel. Indeed, in 1950, before Vatican II, this was the first and only house in Iloilo where priests could celebrate the mass, as Pope Pius XII had granted Agatona a papal bull allowing her to build a private chapel in her residence.

It was also around this time that the house was partially reconstructed, having been bombed by the Japanese during the Second World War. Cherished heirlooms, including statues of saints and other religious relics, are kept under glass. The precious tableware appropriated by the Japanese during the war, when they occupied the house, had to be bought back. Other antique dining sets as well as silverware are either proudly displayed or jealously guarded.

Today, externally, the house looks quite different from how it did originally. The ground floor has been mostly converted into commercial space, and the building blends in well with the hive of activity that the area has become. It is when one enters, through the remaining "cathedral" doors, that the full force of history and tradition hits.

Past the cavernous foyer that serves as a receiving room, one ascends the lower flights of an imperial staircase to a landing where a life-size effigy of Our Lady of the Candles is encased in the wall behind glass. This statue, which

is considered miraculous, only leaves the house for Jaro Cathedral once a year, on the shoulders of eight people, where it is kept overnight until the annual Jaro Fiesta on 2 February, when she is paraded through the streets of the district on a *carroza* (horse-drawn carriage).

The final flight of steps leads to the main *sala* dominated by the private chapel on the left, the entrance of which mimics an ancient Roman temple with a heavy pediment on Corinthian-capital pilasters. Century-old church kneelers once used by Agatona in Jaro Cathedral stand before the main altarpiece, a statue of Christ the King. Back in the *sala*, a life-size portrait of Agatona looms over an ornate 1950s sofa, upholstered in brocade and positioned across from four armchairs from the same set.

Stationed against the opposite wall is an opulent Ah-Tay bed (a Chinese furniture manufacturer fashionable during the late 1800s and early 1900s) that once belonged to owner Regina "Jean" Jalandoni's maternal grandfather. All around the room are family photographs and paintings, interspersed with religious objects including a replica of the original stone statue of Our Lady of the Candles that now sits atop Jaro Cathedral.

Blue, liturgical green and yellow are the dominant decorative colours, lifting the heavy, dark wood around

the house. These can be found in the semicircular fanlight windows that match the frosted green windowpanes. They also appear between the door frames leading to the kitchen and informal dining area, and again in the glass above the double doors accessing the *volada* – an enclosed gallery running along the sides of the dining room. The dining room itself is austere, despite the playful curves on the cream-coloured chairs of the dining table that seats 18.

Wealth, derived from both property and sugar, combined with a deep devotion to the Catholic faith drove Agatona's philanthropy, the main beneficiaries of which were the priests and nuns who lived out their vocation in the Archdiocese of Jaro. She lived until 90, but long before then the mantle had safely passed to her nephew, whom she and her husband, Ruperto Lopez Jalandoni (they were childless), adopted: Carlos Liberata Jalandoni, the orphaned son of her brother Fausto.

Adored by his adoptive parents, Carlos would grow up to be a sharp businessman. He also inherited Agatona's deep commitment to the Church, serving as co-Chairman of the powerful Bishops-Businessmen's Conference. He was

My grandmother was very motherly. Even when she was mostly bedridden, she would always ask for us. I remember how on my sixth birthday I didn't want to be with the guests. So she just sat with me, the whole time, there on the sofa.

Regina "Jean" Jalandoni

supported by his wife, the equally devout Cecilia Montinola Jalandoni, whose every wish he granted but who, if her advice fell on her husband's deaf ears, would speak to him via a monsignor or bishop ("Monsignor, please tell Charlie to do this …").

Indeed, for the clergy based in or passing through Iloilo, including the splendidly named Cardinal Sin, the Arguelles-Jalandoni residence was a veritable open house, with a cook who knew their favourite foods and the promise of a well-stocked bar.

Many of Carlos' responsibilities have now passed on to Jean, one of Carlos and Cecilia's five children who grew up in the house – her siblings being Jose Maria, Rose Marie, Carlos Jr and Miguel Angel (who died when he was five). When

their Lola was alive but mainly confined to her bed, Jean remembers having to creep into her bedroom next to the chapel before going out to play in the town plaza. Agatona's nurse would dole out their allowance – a then generous 25 centavos – and permission would be granted on condition that they returned when the cathedral bells rang six o'clock and it was time to say the Angelus. When the chapel was constructed, a connecting door was built to allow Agatona to hear mass from the comfort of her room.

Although none of the family actually live in the house any longer, the reverence for tradition endures, including hosting an elaborate lunch during the Jaro Fiesta. Jean has also realised her mother's dream of setting up, on family land, a chapel and convent dedicated to Saint Padre Pio of Pieltrecina.

When we were small, we thought the dining room was untouchable because we were not allowed to sit at the table with my grandmother, who always invited priests and nuns to have lunch with her every Sunday. We only found out later that my grandmother did want us to join them, but only after we had received our First Holy Communion.

Regina "Jean" Jalandoni

HORMILLOSA-LOCSIN
HOUSE

Jaro, Iloilo City

A Curated Residence

Those in search of unique architectural accoutrements could do worse than be invited
into the Hormillosa-Locsin mansion in Jaro.

Ownership of this turn-of-the-century domicile has passed on to the heirs of the late Leopoldo Hormillosa-Locsin II, whose widow, Remia Gimena Locsin, is the consummate guide to this impeccably maintained, beautifully decorated *bahay na bato* home.

She points out the fan-shaped, *abanico* staircase in the stone passageway, with its broad winders, linking the ground floor to the *entresuelo*, or mezzanine; in terms of domestic architecture, it is the only one of its kind in Iloilo. In addition, upstairs the carved wooden arches (*calados*) that decorate and at the same time signify the separation of rooms feature fern-like leaves – an element not normally found, if at all, in other Iloilo homes.

What also distinguishes this ancestral house is the way in which the owner's finely tuned sense of style has been able to create an attractive "stage" combining family heirlooms with pieces she has introduced herself over the past four decades. This is, after all, the house where her husband, Leopoldo, grew up and where she has lived continuously since the 1980s.

His grandparents, Leopoldo Hormillosa and Froilana Jalandoni Hormillosa, were the original owners of the house. The family's extensive business interests ranged from sugar to tobacco. During the Second World War, the Japanese forces were said to have found the residence only attractive enough to use as a kitchen. Fast-forward a few years, and a framed certificate in the house today attests to the older Leopoldo's donation of the then princely sum of 500 pesos to the inauguration of the Republic of the Philippines on 4 July 1946.

Leopoldo and Froilana had four children. One of their daughters, Corazon Hormillosa Locsin, married Manuel Locsin and had four children – Leopoldo, Frolu, Dennis and Frankie. A lawyer by profession, Manuel was also a member of a large clan of sugar planters. Both Manuel and his son Leopoldo were keen golfers; according to Remia, working as a farmer held little appeal for the younger Leopoldo.

My father-in-law's original desk is here, as well as his original law books. I want to preserve them. I don't throw things away, especially books from a long time ago.

Remia Gimena Locsin, *owner*

After they met (on a golf course) and married in the 1970s, Remia and Leopoldo lived in Manila, where he was an assemblyman in the Philippine legislature formed in 1978. They moved to Iloilo permanently in 1984 when President Ferdinand Marcos appointed Leopoldo as Governor of Guimaras, an island province south of Panay (the island of which Iloilo is the largest city).

Since then, Remia has lived in the house, raising their children and performing the role of housewife and chatelaine. Now a grandmother, she has converted the large room under the staircase that was once used to store tobacco into a giant playroom for her grandchildren. When Leopoldo died in 2020, he was the Chairman of the Board of the family-owned Janiuay Rural Bank.

As the long-time custodian of the house, Remia's efforts have helped to ensure that the Hormillosa-Locsin House, less than 100 steps from Jaro Cathedral, remains one of Iloilo's best-preserved ancestral homes. That it is bigger than it looks from the outside is indisputable; some of the bedrooms, mostly modernised, could pass for modest-size apartments in themselves.

They will have their chesterfield settee, their
armchairs in soft natural leather as stylish as seats in
Italian racing cars, their rustic tables, their lecterns,
and their fitted carpets, silk rugs, and light oak
bookcases ... They will have china, silver cutlery, lace
napkins, sumptuous red leather bindings.

Georges Perec, *Things. A Story of the Sixties*, translated from the French by
David Bellos, Boston, MA: David R Godine Publisher, Inc., 1990 [1965], p. 125

The stylishness of the interiors can be seen from the upper storey's first public space. The airy anteroom (*caida*) at the top of the stairs is a transformed *volada*. This show-stopping gallery comprises a tastefully curated corner with an intricately carved display cabinet, the first of several antique jars (here, on pedestals) and a woven-rattan (*solihiya*) divan. At the far end of the room, a classic butterfly sofa forms the centrepiece of a relaxed seating area. Lining the walls is a three-seater wooden sofa and tables displaying assorted earthenware, while the centre aisle is flanked by two period mirrors. One is reminded of author Georges Perec's 1960s "hymn" to *les choses* (the things) gracing the Paris residence of his protagonists.

Enclosing this convivial space are multi-coloured window-glass panels – square and diamond-shaped – louvred (*persiana*) windows and the signature sliding *capiz* windows of the Philippine stone house. The striking red-and-white patterned tile floor is original, and while the ceiling has since been refitted with plywood (they had discovered asbestos in the original) its geometric moulding remains the same. Swing doors next to the staircase conceal the family dining room, which adjoins the kitchen – allowing a sense of privacy even if there were visitors in the anteroom.

Beyond the two sets of double doors in the anteroom lies the main living room, the *sala mayor*, furnished in classic-contemporary style, complementing the elements typical of

the period and type of abode. Here are family photographs, more jars, an antique upright piano, paintings, religious-shrine boxes, a set of oil lamps, two sala sets – both with comfortable stuffed sofas – and a regal Venetian mirror. Taken together, they complete the look of an elegant and relaxing salon.

Open double doors lead to a short hallway taking one back to the aforementioned dining room and kitchen. For all her obvious good taste, Remia gamely admits to having been taken to task by her late friend Zafiro Ledesma Jr, then curator of Museo Iloilo, for

the rare decorating misstep, such as painting over the circular cut-outs in the living room's transom windows. She has since restored them to their original, clear state in order to let in the light as they were originally meant to do.

From Remia's kitchen window, one can catch a glimpse of the ruins of an old mansion, now tilting to one side because the owners were digging for gold that they believed had been buried by the Japanese during the war. "High finance" may be how Remia Gimena Locsin describes the demands of running an old house but, by formally taking over the Hormillosa-Locsin ancestral home, she is helping to create a legacy worth so much more than gold.

No one was staying here in the house. My husband's brothers and sisters had their own houses. But I liked this house. It was so nice. I said we would stay here, but little did I know how "high finance" [how expensive] it would be. It sometimes seems easier to build a new house.

Remia Gimena Locsin

PISON
ANCESTRAL HOUSE
Molo, Iloilo City

Solid Socle and Sliding Screens

Art Nouveau-style floral patterns in the soffit vents underneath the eaves contrast with the solid brickwork surrounding the heavy main door.

Set in the middle of a roundabout in Mandurriao, Iloilo City is a dramatic relief sculpture commissioned by the Pison family of Molo. The work of native Iloilo artist Ed Defensor, it illustrates the accomplishments of their enterprising forebear, Donato M Pison Sr. Rising from the chimney of a muscovado mill built by Donato in the 1880s, each of the monument's four sides is dedicated to an industry in which the pioneering farmer and entrepreneur prospered – sugar, rice, fish husbandry and salt-making.

Another monument to Donato Sr's success is the home he built for his wife, Paciencia Tijam Pison, and their family in Molo on a street close to what is now the celebrated Iloilo River Esplanade. A classic *bahay na bato* (literally "house of stone", but referring to Philippine residences with a masonry – i.e. stone or brick – socle or base), the original house was constructed out of bamboo and *nipa* (mangrove palm) in the late 1800s, while its current form dates to 1907.

Today, the house embodies a family's orderly lifestyle and foresight. As an aging widow, Paciencia initiated the equitable division of her assets among her children – Damian, Concepcion, Antonio, Glicerio, Rosario, Donato Jr, Pedro and Severo – thus sparing them from crippling death duties. Even before he married and had a family of his own, Pedro inherited the house and its contents by drawing lots (still a common practice among some old Filipino families). But it was not until the 1950s that Pedro and his wife, Socorro Fuentes Pison, would move into the house. Before then, Pedro was based in Cebu, in the Philippines' Central Visayas region, and afterwards Davao, on the southern island of Mindanao, where he had various business ventures and a number of his children were born. During this period, the house was occupied by his brother Antonio, who was also married to one of his wife's sisters. Another sister, Jovita Fuentes, was an international opera singer and the Philippines' first female National Artist in Music.

Now, even Pedro and Socorro's children – Rosalinda, Victor, Donato III, Cynthia, Edgardo and Delia – have received their inheritances, but their parents' astute investments ensure that none of the offspring has to reach into his or her own pocket to maintain the house, except for the cost of repairs to their own rooms. Utility bills are divided equitably.

The Pison Ancestral House was actually rebuilt after being destroyed during the Japanese occupation of the Philippines in the Second World War. And since the outbreak of the coronavirus pandemic, the dwelling's magnificent frontage – specifically, its upper storey – has been given a fresh coat of white and celadon paint (the

Sliding panels of *capiz* shells framed in a wooden grid, kept out the rain. Inside the *capiz* layer, sliding panels of adjustable wooden louvers *(persiana)* screened away the heat of the sun while allowing currents of cooling air to enter the house. The elaborate window system continued down to the floor [with the *ventanilla:* the so-called "little window"] Under the wooden sill which held up a double layer of sliding panels, followed by a set of *persiana,* and finally guarded by wooden balusters on the exterior.

Augusto F Villalón, *Lugar: Essays on Philippine Heritage and Architecture*, Makati: Bookmark, Inc., 2001, p. 28

We have had an unbroken series of family reunions since 1936. My great-grandmother set the date which is actually Labour Day. She recognised we had to have a reunion for the farmhands, to show them that we are all together in this, and as a tribute to them.

Kevin Pison Piamonte, *great-grandson of Donato and Paciencia Pison*

latter providing the colour scheme that flows into the *entresuelo*, or mezzanine, and upwards into the *caida*, or anteroom, and *sala mayor*, the main living room).

It is in the upper storey that this house really excels, and provides an almost textbook example of the sophisticated sliding-screen elevations developed in the Philippines – so redolent of Japanese *shoji* architecture rather than any Iberian or Caribbean "Antillan" antecedents.

To reach the living quarters upstairs, one must pass the *zaguan cuadra* (space for carriages and religious floats), which now serves as a garage. Here, the Pisons provided shelter to the Lenten *caruaje* (carriage) of another old Molo family, the Sians, whose life-size image of the Santo Entierro, the dead Christ, was revered during processions held on Good Friday. Even the sight of the carriage would give Kevin Piamonte – great-grandson of Donato and Paciencia, and an

award-winning filmmaker – a terrible fright each time he visited the house.

The house's *caida* and *sala mayor* are relatively spartan, albeit elegantly furnished with formal wooden sofas, cane and wooden arm- and rocking chairs, antique camphor-wood chests, display cabinets and pedestals. Broad floorboards of apitong (a kind of Southeast Asian hardwood) sourced from, Kevin says, "ruined bridges and wooden ships" from the wharf in nearby La Paz run the length of the room. Family photographs adorn the walls of the anteroom, including those of the original inhabitants and their children.

Three features stand out in the *sala mayor*: a 100-year-old wooden sofa with a sign imploring visitors not to sit on it; the striking figure of a stylised butterfly carved into a window colonette; and the likeness of Filipino national hero José Rizal tucked among the leafy, Art Nouveau shapes

I feel I have become an artist because of my grandmother, Socorro. She had a beautiful voice ... I remember her standing by the window and singing the aria "Un bel di vedremo" from *Madame Butterfly* for me.

Kevin Pison Piamonte

of the wooden *sala* arch. Apparently, Rizal used to visit the Pisons' neighbours, the Lazaros, next door, but Kevin believes its existence owes more to the fact that his great-grandfather Donato and Rizal were both Freemasons.

Tall double doors to the right of the emphatic, double-flight staircase lead to a comfortable *comedor*, or dining room. Rosalinda recalls how her Papa, Pedro, would enjoy orange marmalade and toast for breakfast, and how as children they were never allowed to leave the table while the adults, particularly the head of the household, were still eating.

The Pisons, like many established planter families, revered two things above all else: family and education. "Our grandmother was a widow for 18 years, and she managed to send four of her children to school abroad," says Rosalinda, "Papa went to UC Berkeley, and the others went to Stanford and New York University." Her sister Cynthia Pison de Leon adds, "Our father told us, 'Don't depend on the land. Depend on what we will be giving you – an education.' This is why we all work."

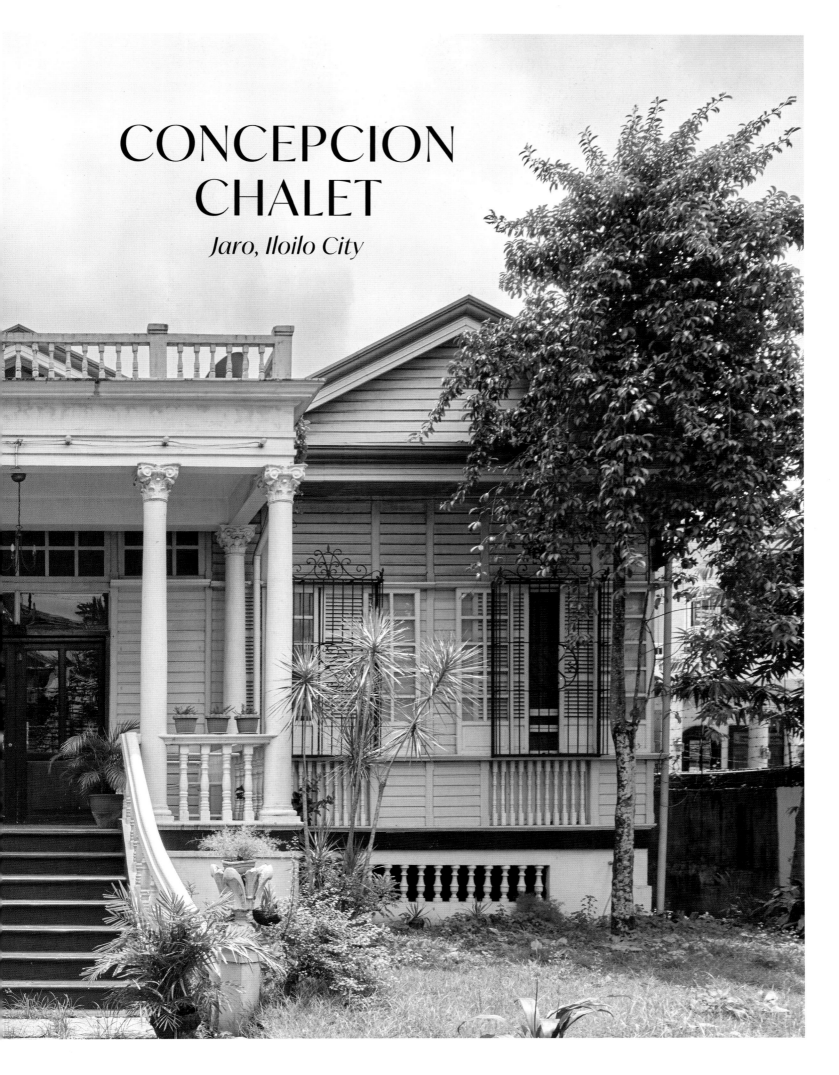

CONCEPCION CHALET

Jaro, Iloilo City

The "One Square Cabin"

There was a time, it is said, when the streets of Iloilo were lined with chalets, pronounced "tsa-lets" in the phonetic Spanish way. Most were destroyed during the Second World War, so that the Concepcion Chalet in the district of Jaro remains one of the rare examples of the genre left in the city today.

*T*his *"modern Philippine architecture" must have caught the fancy of Attorney Jose Poblador Concepcion, Sr [such] that in 1924 he built a chalet across [from] the Ledesma ancestral home for his wife Rosalina Benedicto Ledesma, along Washington Street. Made of hardwood milled from the original floor planks of the old house across the street, the modest structure had rooms that opened to public spaces with hand carved filigree cutwork and encaustic cement tiles (from the Machuca Tile Company that had opened in 1900) sporting decorative foliage in the Art Nouveau and Art Deco styles.*
- E Jamerlan, "The Concepcion Chalet", *The News Today*, 10 May 2010. Available online at https://www.thenewstoday.info/2010/05/14/the.concepcion.chalet.html

Built in 1924 by Jose Poblador Concepcion Sr, a lawyer, and his wife, Rosalina Ledesma Concepcion, the Concepcion Chalet was of a style made popular in the early 1900s, the first part of the American colonial era. This "one square cabin" structure, referencing the shape of the dwelling, formed an unassuming counterpoint to the lavish mansions sprouting up across Jaro and Molo. But for the chalet's typical owner – middle-class entrepreneurs, well-educated professionals and even members of the landed gentry – their home did not imply any architectural comedown.

Rather, the chalet represented a step forward from the early *bahay na bato* in terms of its reassuring distance from the street and the availability of modern amenities such as

They say this is one of two remaining chalets in Iloilo. Professors of architecture visit this house, and I learn from their lectures. They choose to come to Iloilo because they say it is complete in terms of demonstrating the evolution of Philippine architecture.

Cynthia Concepcion Baga, *granddaughter of Jose and Rosalina Concepcion*

During the war at first we stayed at home. When they bombed the depot, our father told us to hide under the table. We fled, pushing a cart with all our things. We joined other families, and lived in a *nipa* hut.

Jose Concepcion Jr, *son of Jose and Rosalina Concepcion*

electrical wiring and plumbing. Here, indoor and even en-suite bathrooms were the norm. In this respect, they were the equals of the larger homes equipped with the latest technologies.

The three-bedroom Concepcion Chalet was built on land that had belonged to Rosalina's parents – Modesto Ledesma, a sugar planter of substantial means, and Librada Benedicto Ledesma. Cynthia Concepcion Baga, their granddaughter and recognised "keeper of the family narrative", remembers the house once being surrounded by a beautiful Classical garden, complete with paved concrete path – but these features, together with three front steps, have been completely obliterated by flooding over the years.

Otherwise, the house has been carefully preserved. The American influence is seen in the double-fronted, timber-boarded symmetrical façade boasting twin gables and a central porch integrating Neoclassical accents – among them, two pairs of slender Corinthian-capital columns

holding aloft a flat roof. A third gable is just visible behind the central parapet.

Inside, sliding *capiz*, glass-panelled and louvred windows combine with floor-level *ventanillas* to stimulate air circulation and ventilation. Art Nouveau-style decorative arches running along the slatted ceiling and separated by a central post divide the open-plan living space from the dining room. While Jose Sr and Rosalina's daughters – Ofelia, Marina, Elisea, Pilar and Cecile – occupied a bedroom that shares a wall with the formal living room located on the left of the house, both the master's bedroom and the room of the boys – Jose Jr and Alberto – were located on the right.

Perhaps because of the house's size and relative informality, the children and adults grew up in close proximity, and the dwelling still emits an air of amiability and candour. The history of the house and how it came to be built is now an open family secret.

The eldest of 10 children, Rosalina displayed an independent streak, following her heart to marry a young journalist and aspiring lawyer of whom her parents disapproved because he was a "mere" professional. As one of Cynthia's aunts explained to her, "Your Lolo [Grandfather] did not want your mother to marry your father because he was worried he couldn't afford her." When Cynthia pointed out that he was a professional, her aunt countered, "But

you don't inherit anything from professionals. You hire them!" In other words, Jose Sr was not – *apart* from being a lawyer – a *haciendero*.

The young couple eloped, with the help of one of Rosalina's maternal aunts, and settled in Manila. As Marina Concepcion Yvanovich, Jose Sr's second daughter (then 99 years of age), recalled in 2019, "Later on, when our grandfather saw how much our parents loved each other,

he accepted the marriage." Life in Manila proved challenging for the young couple, but it was only after the death of their firstborn son, Ruben, that they returned to Iloilo, where Jose Sr, now a fully fledged lawyer and notary public, was made the administrator of Modesto's farms. The couple were also gifted their own *hacienda*. Rosalina proved to be extremely enterprising and, discovering a fondness for jewellery among her relatives and friends, started a successful jewellery business – at first carrying the precious wares around in her handbag. The business is now a successful third-generation enterprise.

The Concepcion Chalet has outlasted the "father house", a sprawling estate built by Modesto Ledesma in 1936, which has since been sold. Marina remembered the generosity of her mother – how she enjoyed the odd cigarette and glass of wine, and her penchant for hosting parties in the chalet complete with live bands and dancing. "Whenever she made money, she made sure we enjoyed it, instead of using that money to buy a building or lot. Life for us was very easy. After liberation from the Japanese, she sent me and my sister to Japan on American President Lines. She did whatever made us happy."

The house today serves as the structural heart of the family, where Cynthia, a psycho-spiritual formation specialist, makes sure that every Sunday lunch is an "open house" for family. Although it is now owned by Rosalina and Jose Sr's eldest grandchild, Antonio "Tony" Concepcion Pastelero, it is still very much a family hub. As his uncle Alberto "Bert" Concepcion says, "We make sure to hold all celebrations here. It makes the house come alive."

In April 2023, Marina Yvanovich passed away peacefully, but the life of the house will continue – a tribute to the indomitable spirit of a proud Ilonggo family.

I asked an aunt why do we only have a chalet? She said, Of course, because your parents had to work hard in order to build the house, the two of them [Rosalina and Jose Sr] in tandem. So in this house, the old floors in the living room were plaster wood from Modesto's *bodega,* which they bought from him. They also had winnings from "monte" [a card game]. With this and their savings they were able to build this house.

Cynthia Concepcion Baga

NELLY GARDEN

Jaro, Iloilo City

A House for Performance

Iloilo boasts many imposing ancestral homes constructed by landed families when Philippine sugar was at its peak, but even their proudest heirs might be forgiven for pointing to Nelly Garden as the jewel in the crown.

Set back from a busy main road traversing the districts of La Paz and Jaro, the Neoclassical, colonial-style mansion built by Vicente Villanueva Lopez and his wife, Elena Hofileña Lopez, embodies all the glory and grandeur of an era.

The property was designed as an unusually modern reinforced-concrete structure by engineer Mariano Salas, who also built fellow sugar planter Celso Ledesma's "Eagle house" across the city. Sitting on two hectares of prime real estate, Nelly Garden's main house dominates a wide stretch of lawn flanked by mature tropical trees. Regarding its supremely orchestrated entrance façade, Augusto Villalón waxes lyrical:

The facade is topped by a gentle, peineta*-shaped arch (Spanish ornamental comb) whose surfaces are frosted with concrete*

filigree so delicate it seems to have been piped in by a cake decorator. A gentle cap of assorted, feathery finials completes it, bringing the focus to a protruding central volume consisting of a second-story balcony above the main, ceremonial house entrance.
- Augusto F Villalón, "Peeling Away Layers of Ilonggo Architecture", in A. Feleo (ed.), *Iloilo: A Rich and Noble Land*, Metro Manila: Lopez Group Foundation, 2007, p. 105

In this house were raised Vicente and Elena's four children and two cousins. The eldest, named after her mother and doted on by her father, lent her nickname, "Nelly", to the house. Her siblings were Vicente Jr, Benito and Lilia; raised alongside them were their first cousins – Eugenio and Fernando Hofileña Lopez. Vicente had become the boys' guardian after the assassination of their father, his older brother Benito. Eugenio would go on to build the famous Boat House nearby.

By the time the family moved into Nelly Garden, Vicente was already one of Iloilo's most prominent businessmen, a civic leader and philanthropist. An invitation to one of the Lopezes' formal parties was a mark of one's political and business influence – and social cachet. Important guests from Manila and abroad, including members of the diplomatic corps, would be driven up to the main entrance

porch, the doors flung open to reveal an expansive space meant for performance and dancing. One is reminded of Canadian writer Michael Ondaatje's description of the dramatic houses of his family's native Sri Lanka:

The walls, painted in recent years a warm rose-red, stretch awesome distances away to my left to my right and up towards a white ceiling ... The doors are twenty feet high, as if awaiting the day when a family of acrobats will walk from room to room, sideways, without dismantling themselves from each other's shoulders.
- Michael Ondaatje, *Running in the Family,* London: Picador, 1984 [1982], p. 24

For Francesca ("Frannie") Jison Golez, great-granddaughter of Vicente, the corner of the *sala* where stands a Steinway grand piano is her favourite spot, just by the bronze bust

of the patriarch by Filipino National Artist in Sculpture Guillermo Tolentino. Perched on the lid is an iconic photograph of the musical Lopez children: Nelly, on the harp; Lilia, on the piano; Vicente, on cello; and Benito, on the violin.

The intricately carved arches framing the living-room ceiling are original – made from narra wood. The tindalo floors are also as laid in 1928, while the opulent Chinese blackwood furniture with inlaid mother-of-pearl post-dates the Second World War – when the family indulged their passion for Oriental antiques on trips to Hong Kong. Portraits of Vicente and Elena painted by Fernando Amorsolo (regarded as the "Grand Old Man of Philippine Art") sit on the faux fireplace, while those of their children and grandchildren hang on adjacent wood-panelled walls. Across the room, an antique wall telephone turns out to be part of Lilia Lopez Jison's toy collection.

A professional-size billiard table crafted by the House of Puyat (the furniture empire started with Gonzalo Puyat building his first billiard table) anchors one corner of this large space. A globe drinks trolley, complete with cut-glass decanters, stands nearby at the far wall, completing the impression of an open-plan games room.

The house almost did not survive the Second World War. Filipino guerrillas (resistance fighters against the Japanese) had been given orders to burn it down to keep it from being taken over by the invaders. The story goes that the guerrillas were too busy looting the premises to hear the Japanese soldiers march in and take over. Vicente's daughter, now Lilia Lopez Jison, and her husband, Francisco Lopez Jison, are said to have begged the guerrillas to spare the house. "We lost many family scrapbooks as these were used for target practice by the Japanese," says Francesca.

Lilia and Francisco eventually took over the property. Both now deceased, they had three children: Elena (Elen) Lopez Jison Golez, Francesca's mother; Francisco Jr; and Lourdes Lopez Ledesma. While Lourdes still exercises overall control over the urban estate from her home in Bacolod, it is Frannie – a US-educated graphic designer, social entrepreneur and keen environmentalist – who lives in Nelly Garden, where she grew up with her three younger sisters Lilian, Cecilia and Isabel.

Now almost 100 years since it was built, Nelly Garden is a much sought-after venue for weddings and concerts. A gallery separates the lower, curved level of the L-shaped staircase from the higher steps leading to the upper hallway. Here, the Lopezes would seat the matriarchs during reunions of the wider Lopez clan, as well as principal guests

Lilia Lopez Jison loved being around people, and she would really get a kick out of watching them at these parties. They lived a gracious lifestyle, with the bougainvillea flowers at the centre of the long table, and where the waiters wore gloves and the ladies serving were in black with white aprons.

Narzalina Lim, *friend of Elen Jison Golez*

at various events. All furniture would be cleared from the living room below and the main programme would begin, featuring dances or musical performances. Narzalina Lim, a close friend of Elena, remembers how much Lilia would enjoy watching the *cotillons* (balls) taking place below.

Francesca recalls her Lola Lilia in later life choosing to use the formal dining room for daily meals (instead of the less formal breakfast room) where one was surrounded by glass cabinets filled with crystal and antique Noritake porcelain, and where she was served by her personal butler.

Upstairs, the bedrooms are located on both sides of a wide family hallway. At the top of the stairs was the master bedroom, and here one sees the first of several four-poster beds. A headless mannequin displays a gown by famous Filipino couturier Pitoy Moreno, worn by Elena when she was crowned "Queen of Jaro" in 1969. A large photograph of Elena, which once featured in Philippine *Tatler* magazine, dominates the hall, with its Lladró figurines, tapestries and shelves of family photo albums.

All bedrooms share wide "Jack and Jill" Art Deco-inspired bathrooms, innovative for their day, with separate toilets and shower rooms behind doors, and a bath at the centre. These would not be out of place in a 21st-century grand hotel.

Francesca feels that she too has much invested in Nelly Garden. "The house is one big story. You can take your piece of it, and it will talk back to you. Families have a responsibility to preserve what is here and what is left of the past. What some people may throw away, because they think it is worthless, I see so much value and history."

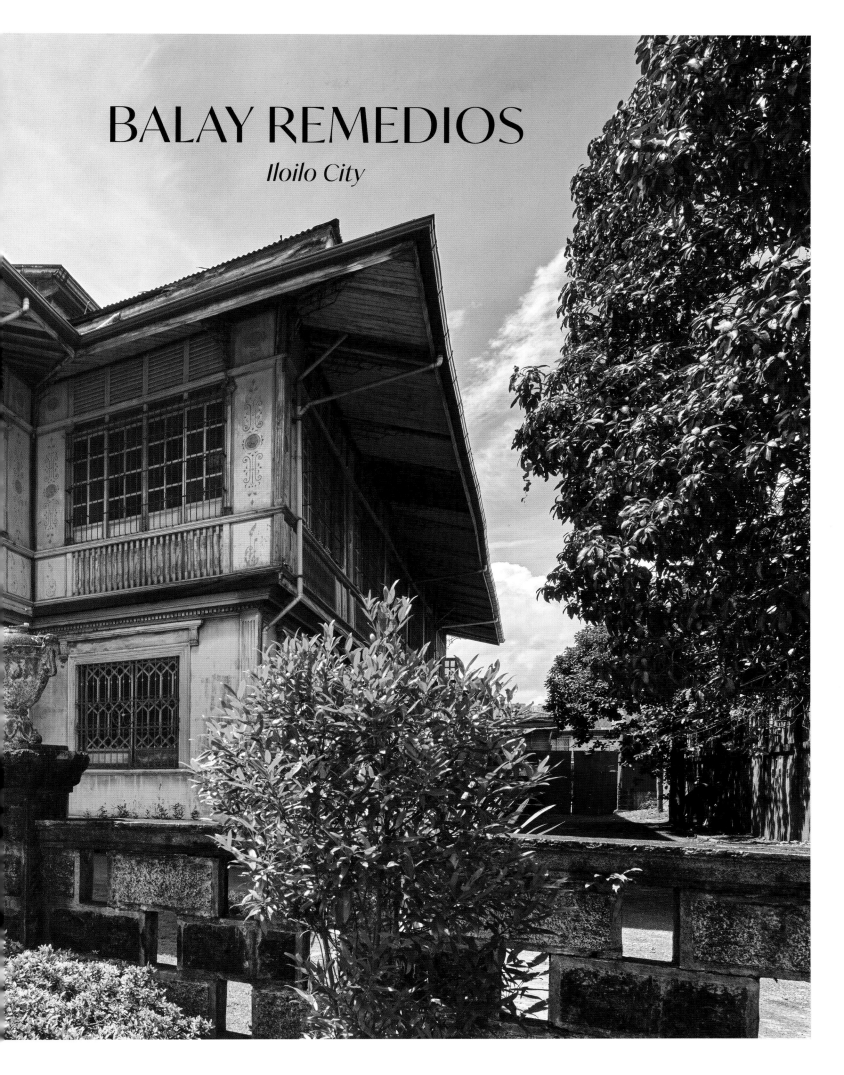

BALAY REMEDIOS

Iloilo City

The Latest from Europe

At one time, unless one was granted special permission, it was nearly impossible to enter the timber-and-concrete mansion situated opposite Museo Iloilo in the city's historic business district.

For years, the house, designed and constructed by the engineer Eusebio Conlu Villanueva in 1917, was left silent and unoccupied save for the discreet presence of a long-time caretaker and her family.

All that changed in the latter half of 2022, however, when Eusebio's youngest daughter – the unmarried Julianita, who had inherited the house from her father – passed away, leaving the mansion to four Villanueva nephews, the sons of her brother Rafael. Now those heirs – led by Gerardo Antonio "Tony" Padilla Villanueva, closely supported by his wife Rosario, or "Charito" – are losing no time making plans to adapt this partly Art Nouveau gem to the needs of a new generation.

They would like the house to be known as Balay Remedios, after their grandmother, Remedios Melliza Sian

When the house was built, Art Nouveau was still the fashion, but times were already moving towards streamline modern. The introduction of styles was not abrupt; they appeared gradually. Here you can tell from the curvilinear flow of the banister of the panelled staircase, and the inverted milk-glass skyscraper pendant lights in the ceiling.

Eugene Jamerlan, *heritage researcher, Iloilo representative for the Philippine Heritage Charter*

While her husband, Eusebio, and his brother Serafin would be known as the "Building Kings" of Iloilo, owning several commercial buildings on adjoining Iznart and J M Basa Streets (the latter, once known as Calle Real: Iloilo's "Royal Road"), Remedios was the true *haciendera*.

Villanueva, whose family – originally from Molo, Iloilo – had sugar lands in Negros Occidental and a muscovado mill in Tigbauan, Iloilo Province.

The house is full of surprises. Its delicately patterned timber panelling and Japanese-style sliding screens belie a modern, concrete structural frame. Here, too, we have the starkest expression of the *porte-cochère* – positioned front and centre rather than tucked away at the side, giving the entrance façade a radically slender, stepped-back appearance in comparison with other Iloilo mansions. Furthermore, the whole ensemble is designed around a modern circulation system, with "In" and "Out" gates; a short, crisp driveway serving the entrance porch; and a long, looping drive continuing on to a private family parking area at the rear of the plot.

In these and several other ways, the dwelling is an expression of its businessman builder's taste, gleaned

from participation in the 20th-century equivalent of the European Grand Tour and other trips – travel, sometimes for as long as six months at a time, being the only true luxury that the Villanuevas, never otherwise extravagant, afforded themselves.

Not surprisingly then, in layout, circulation and detailed design, Balay Remedios represents the "latest from Europe" – a continent at the time awash with radical, new ideas. Perhaps the most obvious manifestation of this tendency is the house's biggest surprise: the switch from plainly panelled ground-floor salons to restrained but extensive Art Nouveau panelling in the enormous, full-depth first-floor hall. These painted and carved hardwood "screens" display stylised flower forms with historian Nikolaus Pevsner's "long, sensitive curve" (a hallmark of this refined style), with floral designs even carrying on to some

of the more public tall doors. As if this were not enough, the ceiling lights throughout shade into the later Art Deco style, with ingenious designs reminiscent of inverted, crystalline skyscraper forms – a transition succinctly noted by Scottish historian Rudolph Kenna:

The early Art Deco style … was seen at its most sumptuous at the Paris Exposition des Arts Decoratifs of 1925 – the show which gave Art Deco its name. Towards the end of the decade the stylised human and animal forms, floral motifs and curvilinear shapes characteristic of mid-Twenties' Art Deco were largely superseded by quasi-Egyptian motifs and hard angular shapes, derived from Cubist and Abstract painting and the chevrons and zigzag patterns of the American skyscraper style (itself deeply influenced by pre-Columbian art).
- Rudolph Kenna, *Glasgow Art Deco,* Glasgow: Richard Drew Publishing, 1985, p. 4

A portrait of Remedios' illustrious ancestor has pride of place on the walls of the residence's newly repainted *sala.* It is also one of the first artefacts that Tony singles out for attention during a tour of the revived mansion. Not many people today realise that Remedios' uncle, Raymundo

... the long, sensitive curve, reminiscent of the lily's stem, an insect's feeler, the filament of a blossom, or occasionally a slender flame, the curve undulating, flowing, and interplaying with others, sprouting from corners and covering asymmetrically all available surfaces, can be regarded as the leitmotif of Art Nouveau ...

Nikolaus Pevsner, *Pioneers of Modern Design*, Harmondsworth: Penguin Books, 1960 [1949], p. 90

> My Lola was a good businesswoman. If she needed to, she'd go to the farm, she'd visit the tenants of her buildings and she'd leave the younger children to her oldest daughter, Violeta, who was more or less a surrogate mother to her brothers and sisters. That's why my Dad, even in his later years, used to call my Tita Vi "Mommy"
>
> Gerardo Antonio "Tony" Padilla Villanueva, *owner*

Angulo Melliza, was a member of the Supreme Court of Cuba; a classmate of King Alfonso XIII of Spain, where he had gone to study; and a good friend of Filipino national hero José Rizal. In fact, Rizal would often visit her uncle in their family house (burnt down during the Second World War) in Molo. Raymundo also has the distinction of being the second Governor of Iloilo and vice presidential candidate during the Philippine general elections of 1935. When he died childless, most of his wealth was inherited by his sister Juliana, mother of Remedios and great-grandmother of Tony Villanueva and his three brothers Sabino, Eusebio Ramon and Rafael.

Their Lolo Eusebio Villanueva originally built the Iloilo mansion as the residence of sugar planter Julio Ledesma – but years later, in 1928, he purchased the house for himself. While it had initially been meant as an investment, that same year he would make it his family home. There he and Remedios would raise their seven children: Violeta, Jose, Francisco, Rafael, Solange, Cornelio and Julianita. Eusebio and Remedios lived in the house until 1978, when they decided to move permanently to Negros – from where Eusebio continued to run his many Panay businesses, albeit remotely. But as a boy, during the school holidays, Tony would often visit the house in Iloilo, where his father, Rafael, was still based.

Charito says that the family actually had very little furniture considering the scale of the rooms, the walls of which, downstairs at least, have been refreshed in shades approximating their original colours: salmon pink in the main *sala*, a dark-green palette in the chapel off the *sala*, yellow in the main dining room and mocha in what used to be Eusebio's receiving room. The four bedrooms (so large that they each have two double-height doors) in the private quarters above have yet to be restored.

Tony is considering how the house might be transformed into an event space, and already contemplating building a new kitchen on the 1,753 square metre property, with the view to installing a café. There are also plans to create a museum in what used to be his grandfather's room. The new heirs are determined to keep the house they inherited, and all its legacies, alive.

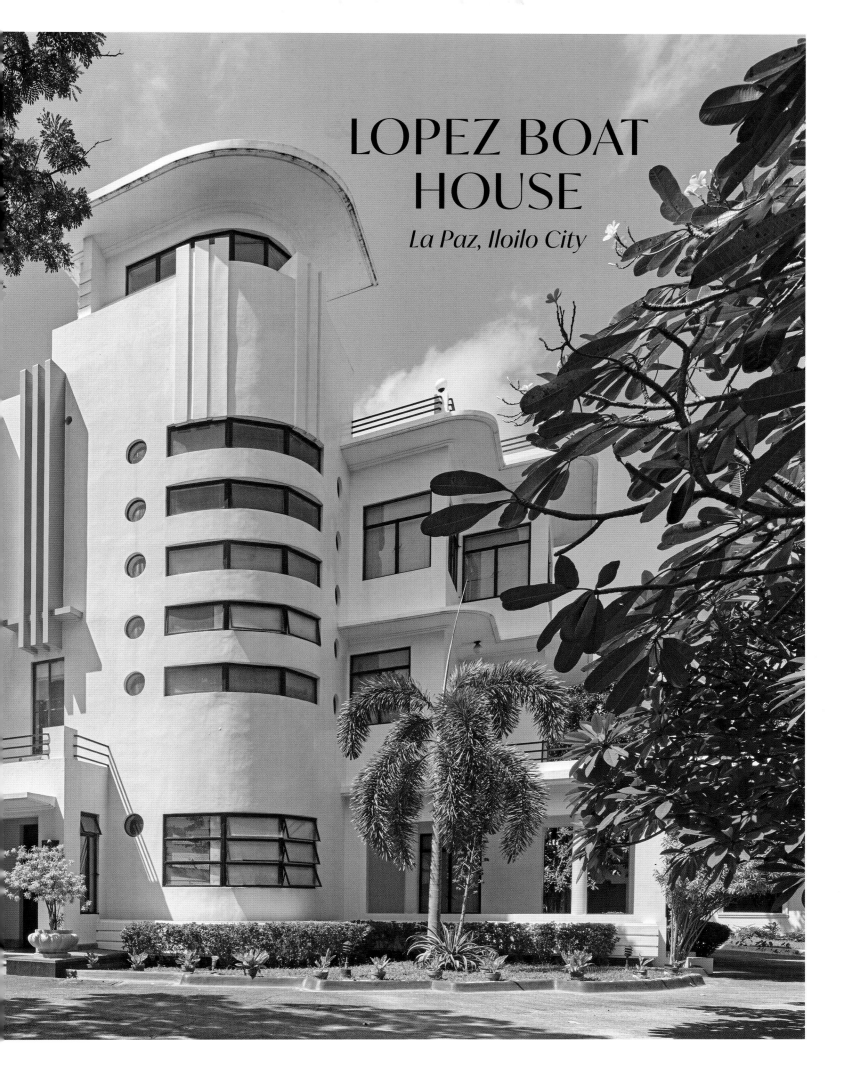

LOPEZ BOAT HOUSE

La Paz, Iloilo City

A Lasting Legacy

This house's Art Deco architecture complements its spectacular interiors, notably the 1930s-style furniture.

I n August 1936, Eugenio "Eñing" Hofileña Lopez Sr threw a party to celebrate two family milestones: the baptism of his only daughter, Presentacion, named after his mother, and the inauguration of his magnificent four-storey Art Deco/Moderne mansion in La Paz, Iloilo. According to the late Raul Rodrigo, the Lopez family's official historian, the celebrations attracted the "cream of Iloilo, Bacolod and Manila society" with President Manuel L Quezon, Eugenio's close friend, acting as the baby's godfather.

Later, Eugenio's son Oscar would describe the house, designed by Manila architect Fernando Ocampo, as looking "like a battleship". Known simply as "Boat House", the Lopez ancestral house stuns with its tower leading to a viewing deck and a ground-floor spiral staircase giving the impression of ascending the levels of a great ocean liner. The late Filipino architect Augusto Villalón commented, in his essay in the book *Iloilo: A Rich and Noble Land*, "Probably the best surviving example of a 1930s art-deco

modern house in the country ... The house makes a superb boat indeed", and noted this nautical style's popularity: "Boathouse is a fine illustration of the era's fascination with streamlined forms associated with speed."

Only 35 years of age and a Harvard-educated lawyer when "Boat House" was built, Eugenio was already at the helm of a business empire spanning land, sea and air transportation; later, he would venture into energy and the media. His savvy propelled the already-prodigious fortunes of the Lopez family of Jaro, Iloilo way beyond sugar and the confines of the Western Visayas. Staying true to his family's origins as planters at the start of the sugar boom in the late 1800s, in the 1950s Eugenio would secure a controlling stake, with other investors, in two of the largest sugar mills in the Philippines – one in Negros Occidental, the other in Pampanga. But by then sugar would be only one of the myriad businesses under his command, with more to come.

Following their father's assassination, Eugenio and his brother Fernando (known as "Nanding") were raised by

their uncle – Vicente Lopez – in the estate now known as "Nelly Garden", not far from Boat House.

Fernando's eldest grandson, Robert "Panchito" Puckett Jr, 75, remembers his grandfather and "Tito" (Uncle) Eñing as being extremely close: "As children, the brothers were inseparable." In fact, for 25 years – between 1947 and 1972 – it was Fernando's immediate family, not Eugenio's, that lived in Boat House.

Architects note : a seaside villa, conceived as are these liners, would be more appropriate than those we see with their heavy tiled roofs.

Le Corbusier, on typical polemical form, in his manifesto, *Vers une architecture*, first published in England by John Rodker in 1927

Eugenio had effectively migrated to Manila with his wife, Pacita Moreno, and their children – Eugenio Jr (known as "Geny"), Oscar, Presentacion, Manuel and Roberto – who grew up there.

Panchito continues, "Fernando Lopez Jr, my Uncle Junjee, was actually the one who lived in Boat House most of the time. But my grandfather and I also lived there.

"Eugenio was very avant-garde and modern. He strove for excellence in everything. He built that very nice, Miami-style art-deco Boat House. Unfortunately, Fernando's house was burnt down by the Japanese during the war, but they spared Boat House because the Japanese turned it into their headquarters."

He says that when Fernando's family occupied Boat House, it was not quite as polished as it looks today – particularly since its restoration in the 1990s by Fernando "Pando"Ocampo Jr, the original architect's son. Says Panchito, "Fernando did not have the same taste as Eugenio. When we lived in Boat House, it was a very spartan house where my grandfather would welcome people from all walks of life. Of course, there was a long table to accommodate different

> My father, Oscar, his siblings and their father as well as their forebears carry a genetic inclination towards being strong nationalists. Their legacy is built on preserving and highlighting the historical, economic and cultural narratives of the nation.
>
> Paz Mercedes "Cedie" Lopez-Vargas, *Executive Director of the Lopez Museum and Library*

people. And the exterior was different then. At the time the façade was all white, without any orange."

From 1992 to 1997, Boat House was occupied by the PAREF Westbridge School, a high school for boys. In 2002, it was declared a Heritage House by the National Historical Commission. Today the house's Art Deco architecture complements its spectacular interiors, notably the 1930s-style furniture. Villalón described the house in its current state in *Iloilo: A Rich and Noble Land*, the impressive tome published by the Lopez Group Foundation:

Flat, plain undecorated walls stretch or bend into curves. Sinuous strips of glass windows combine with portholes. Bedrooms open to flat roof decks. The Boat House vocabulary of shapes captures the romance of ocean liners and the ultramodern optimism of the era. Its recently restored interiors faithfully reinforce the 1930s surroundings with appropriate period furniture, lighting and accessories. What a perfect

backdrop for tuxedos, slinky evening gowns, jazz and smoky rooms to fill out the thirties ambience with human presence that most of the time is missing in Boat House.

The late patriarch of the Lopez clan, Oscar M Lopez's inherited talent for business was only matched by his scholarship and love of history. When his father, Eugenio, founded the Lopez Museum in 1960 to store and share his vast collection of Philippine art, artefacts, rare books, maps and manuscripts with an interested public, Oscar – then a student at Harvard – would scour both rare and popular bookshops looking to buy what he could to add to the museum's collections. His eldest daughter, Paz Mercedes "Cedie" Lopez-Vargas, President of the Lopez Group Foundation and Executive Director of the Lopez Museum and Library, describes her father and forebears' legacy as being built on preserving the Philippines' numerous narratives. Within them, Boat House must surely have its place.

ILOILO

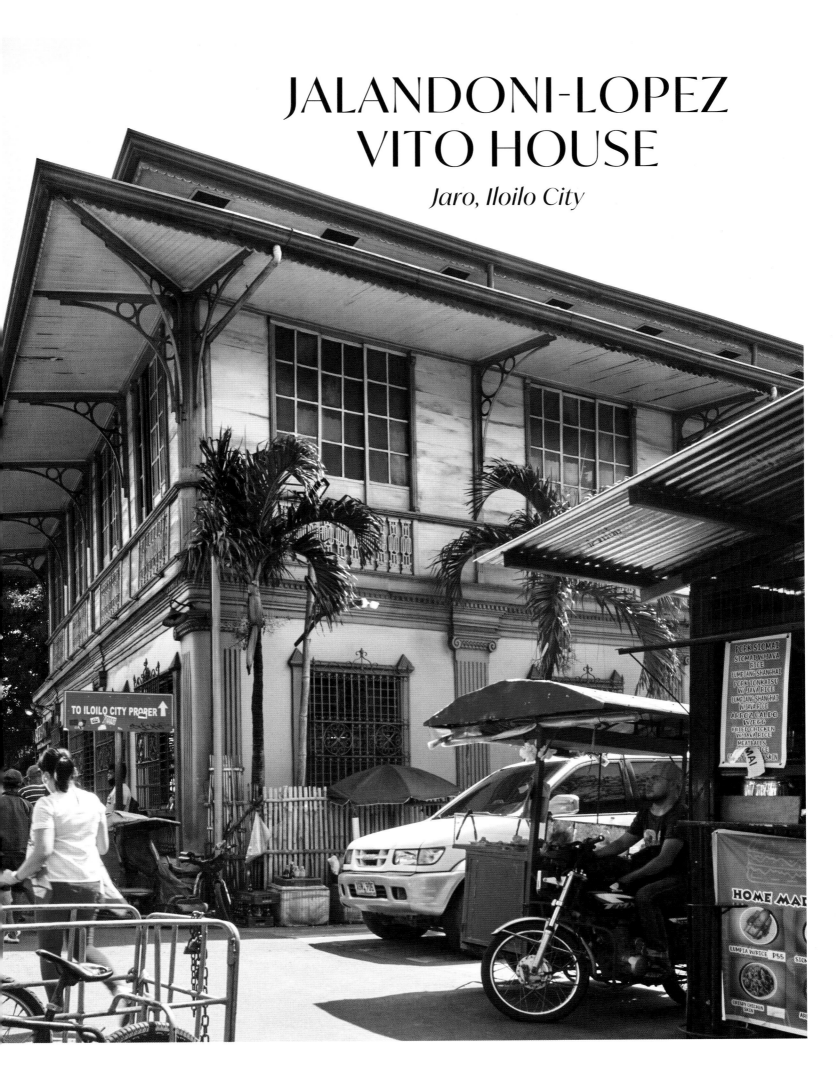

JALANDONI-LOPEZ VITO HOUSE

Jaro, Iloilo City

Honour and Glory

With its "statement" location on the town plaza, flanking the Cathedral of Our Lady of the Candles, this dignified home invites both awe and curiosity. Through the years, it has adapted to the family's domestic needs and those of contemporary living.

Before there ever was an Iloilo City, there was the Roman Catholic Archdiocese of Jaro. Jaro Cathedral, dedicated around 1864 to Our Lady of the Candles, was the first cathedral ever to be built on the island of Panay – emblematic, in all its external Romanesque Revival glory, of the status of this thriving, patrician municipality.

To its left, basking in the afterglow, the *bahay na bato* Jalandoni-Lopez Vito residence originally commanded a clear view of the church from its vast *sala* windows. And while these days the vista may be partially obstructed by other buildings, the mansion still enjoys a "statement" location on the town plaza flanking the cathedral.

The house is accessed via a gate next to Isla Bank, the latter purposefully integrated into the structure. It is one of three branches of the Lopez Vito family-owned thrift bank. On one side of the driveway is an open car garage, on the other a short walkway leading to the door of the main house. According to Rafael "Paeng" Lopez Vito – who lives here with his wife, Maria Flor Jalandoni Lopez Vito – the space now occupied by the bank used to be a stable for the horses while part of the vestibule below the hardwood staircase was allocated to carriages.

The intricately carved balustrades of the house's wide, quarter-turn staircase offer the first glimpse of the fruit and floral flourishes applied to the interiors. The theme extends to the pierced arch hanging above the *sala*, with its repeated blossom and grapevine motifs; it also appears on a floor-level, altar-rail-style divider. Look closely, and the floral accent continues in the curvaceous design of the iron rails encasing the downstairs windows.

The house was originally owned by Rafael's great-grandmother, Eulogia Lopez – one of the daughters of the Lopez clan of Iloilo's progenitor, Basilio – who married Mateo Jalandoni. The property then passed on to one of their daughters, Soledad Lopez Jalandoni. Soledad,

This area was not a *comedor* [dining room], it was a balcony that my grandparents converted. That is why the floor is made of tiles, because it was once open air. You can see the church from here, because the balcony is always supposed to face the church.

Rafael Jalandoni Lopez Vito, *owner*

a spinster, adopted a Jalandoni niece, Remedios, who would inherit the house. Remedios married Jose Ma. Lopez Vito Jr, a lawyer, with whom she had seven children – Jose Manuel, Maria Luisa, Miguel, Rafael, Frankie, Maria Pilar and Jose Maria. Rafael is the current owner of what is now known as the Jalandoni-Lopez Vito House.

At the top of the staircase, the *sala* looms on the right – an epic space, it contains several antiques amassed by Remedios, whose prized acquisitions are kept in the house's museum-like vault.

To the left of the stairs, the railings delineate a relatively informal alcove filled with family portraits, the original cosy dining table and a corner dedicated to Jose Ma. Lopez Vito, Rafael's distinguished grandfather. The elder Lopez Vito held the posts of first Chairman of the Commission on

Elections (Comelec) as well as Governor of both Iloilo and Negros Occidental. Only Rafael, who served as Congressman of the Lone District of Iloilo for eight years, would follow him into politics.

Rafael insists that, substantial though it is, the house is small compared with other would-be ancestral houses. He says he regrets how many of these mansions have disappeared because they have, for various reasons, been demolished, destroyed or simply abandoned to their fate. "But, we know we are lucky to have been able to maintain the house," he says.

The house has adapted to modern times generally; where once *calados* (high-level, pierced transoms), decorative and functional, were deemed sufficient to circulate cool air around the dwelling, air-conditioning units have now been installed – necessitating the fitting of fibre-glass panels

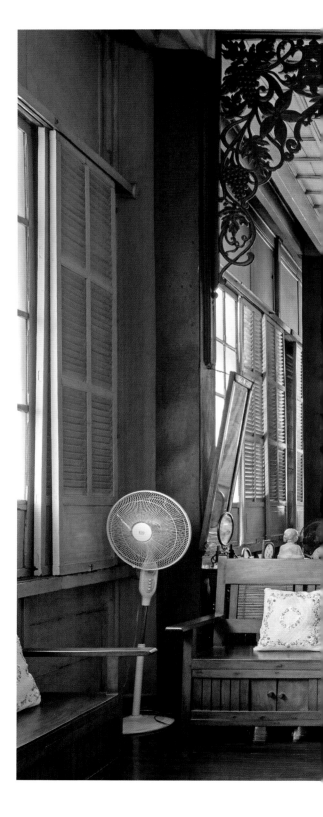

over the comely wooden shapes. Rafael has renovated the master's bedroom, converting two rooms into one and making use of antique wooden posts that had once been kept in the storeroom, or *bodega*.

Among Remedios and Jose's seven children, only Miguel would work on the farm. And while he and all his siblings were raised in a cultured environment ("The older siblings were trained to play an instrument, the younger ones were trained to listen"), the real musical talent belonged to Maria Luisa, who trained under the great Beethoven interpreter Rudolf Serkin, achieving success as a concert pianist and recording artist based in Germany.

Leaving their parents behind in Iloilo, the siblings were sent to study in Manila, where their Lopez Vito grandparents had a house measuring 2,500 square metres in tree-lined New Manila – a prestigious neighbourhood favoured by sugar planters. They would return home for Christmas and the summer holidays.

This is one of the oldest houses here. It was reconstructed and renovated in 1927. I used to have an old picture of the original house which shows that the roof was made of thick *nipa.*

Rafael Jalandoni Lopez Vito

We enjoyed growing up. It was a simple life. Because we were never told that we were privileged. The little money that we were given was just enough for something to eat at school. But I was able to save and go to the movies on Saturday.

Rafael Jalandoni Lopez Vito

The mother superior at our school, Assumption Iloilo, Mother Esperanza, invited us to join her on a trip that lasted three months. In 1961, 20 of us sailed on the Queen Mary *from Southampton to New York after we had travelled around Europe, including Athens and Beirut. At the time, it was peaceful and I loved Beirut. Mother Esperanza allowed us to watch the* Folies Bergère *in Paris. She was liberal and wanted us to experience the world. At the end of the trip, we had to prepare a report.*
- Maria Flor "Mariflor" Jalandoni Lopez Vito

Like many Iloilo sons of his generation, Rafael was enrolled in the Ateneo, a Jesuit-run all-boys school. "Why the Ateneo? I strongly suspect that our parents wanted us to have a more liberal, inclusive education. They taught us to be idealistic; you strive for excellence, for the honour and the glory not, like now, where it is often for the power and the money."

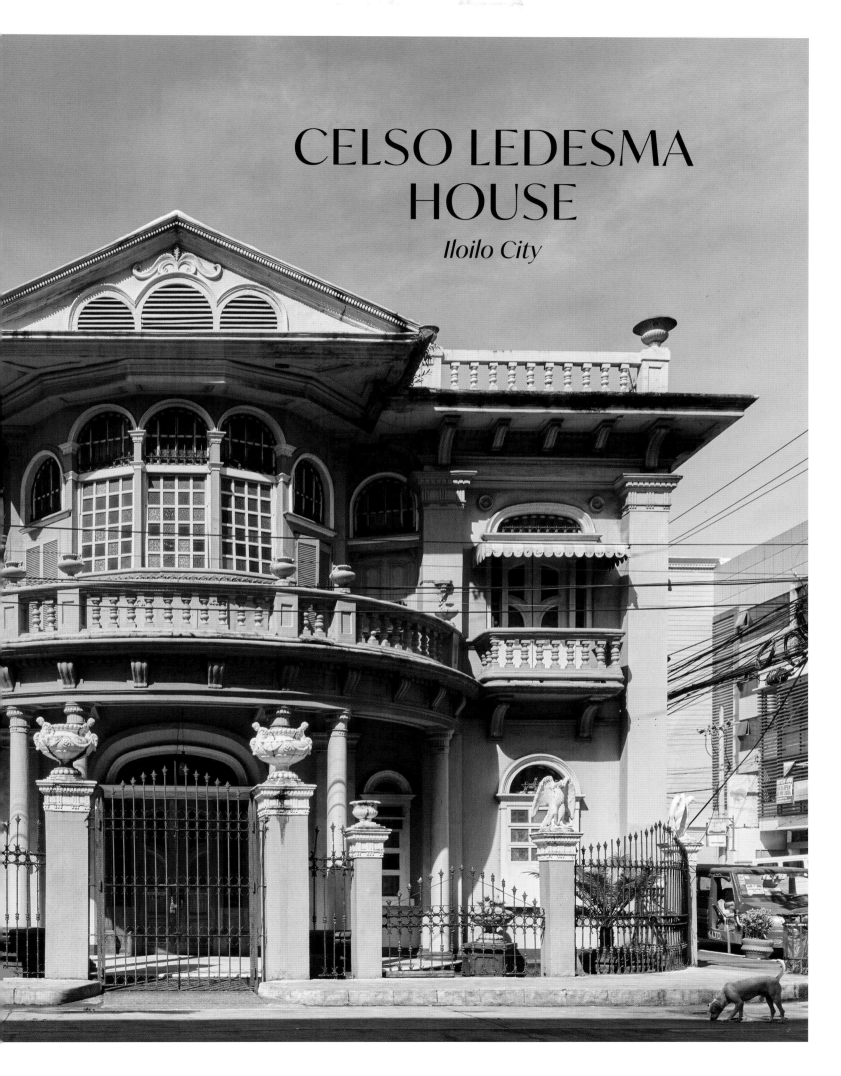

CELSO LEDESMA HOUSE

Iloilo City

A Mannerist Gem

At once stately and playful, traditional and avant-garde, the Celso Ledesma House in the heart of Iloilo's old business district is a fascinating, if perplexing, experience.

*T*hey were sitting in the "landscape-room" on the first floor of the rambling old house on Meng Street … The room was hung with heavy resilient tapestries … They were woven in soft tones to harmonize with the carpet, and they depicted idyllic landscapes in the style of the eighteenth century, with merry vine-dressers, busy husbandmen, and gaily beribboned shepherdesses who sat beside crystal streams.
- Thomas Mann, *Buddenbrooks,* translated from the German by H T Lowe-Porter, London: Secker & Warberg, 1924 [1901], p. 5

Celso Villalobos Ledesma was an inveterate traveller. Having the means to indulge his cultivated tastes, in 1922 he built a spectacular mansion in his home town of Iloilo. Cast-stone eagles standing sentinel along the width of the front gates, Grecian urns beckoning towards the columned portico and main door, the house serves as the perfect expression of the architectural and artistic delights that the globetrotting sugar planter harvested during his travels, many of these extended holidays in Europe.

... hard on the heels of the High Renaissance came the phase known in art
history as "Mannerist", wherein practices which had no ancient Roman precedent
were interspersed among those fully sanctioned, or whole buildings were conceived
in a non-Roman way.

Sir Banister Fletcher's *A History of Architecture*, London: The Athlone Press, 18th edition, 1975, p. 788

A confirmed bachelor, Celso bequeathed the house to his favourite nephew, Tomas Simeon Zafiro Jalbuena Ledesma, known as "Zafiro". Zafiro, who would serve as Mayor of Iloilo City from 1976 to 1979, studied architecture at the University of Santo Tomas in Manila and, as a young man, accompanied his doting, sophisticated uncle on sojourns around the world.

At once stately and playful, traditional and avant-garde, the Celso Ledesma House in the heart of Iloilo's old business district is a fascinating, if perplexing, experience: even his descendants don't know for sure what the true inspirations of its well-travelled patron were.

The ground-floor level – in keeping with the *silong* typology seen also in some Negros dwellings – is almost empty of rooms. One notable exception is the room once inhabited by Zafiro and Gilda, his wife, which leads to a corridor flowing into a space that was once the family-owned bank, managed by Gilda. Before this, the space was open – possibly used as a garage for parking carriages. Patrick Ledesma Jamora, Gilda's son, remembers eating ice cream in the afternoons in his grandparents' room as his Lolo Zafiro sat and smoked (heavily), while on the wall were displayed the propellers of a plane that the patriarch once flew.

Often described architecturally as Beaux Arts, the residence appears to lean equally towards "Mannerist" mores. For every piece of furniture supplied by Gonzalo Puyat & Sons (then the sugar planter's apparent manufacturer of choice), for every Impressionist mural depicting sugar mills or the seasons, there is also an extraordinary feature unique to the house – such as the

horseshoe table and fountain in the dining room, a space daringly balanced above the wide staircase.

The house is planned in a Beaux-Arts manner, it is true, but the designers – local civil engineers M Salas & C Lopez, rather than an architect – skilfully manipulated the layout to incorporate within a nominally symmetrical plan a series of ingenious variations. For instance, a door to the dining room, set in the latter's curving wall, is mirrored not by another doorway but by the blank wall of a projecting bay sheltering a wash-hand basin and a passageway to an external terrace wrapping the room. A landing area in the form of a curved, chapel-style apse is suggested by a sweep of columns, but the space to one side is occupied by a single, deep *sala* while that on the other is divided into an aisle-like passageway and smaller servants' quarters within the same bay depth.

Thus, what seems at first glance to be a straightforwardly Neoclassical arrangement slowly reveals itself to be an almost Mannerist composition – and the effect continues into the decoration of this remarkable space. Heavy wooden cornices are broken into short lengths where interrupted by intervening elements such as curved window heads, and those on either side

of the tall, curved-headed doorways are made to cap projecting bay surfaces in a different-coloured render, tightly hemming the timber-bordered doorways.

The capitals of the columns framing the landing space are formed exclusively from triglyphs and metopes "borrowed" from Ancient Greek temple friezes. These stone decorative devices originally depicted, respectively, wooden beam-ends and the spaces between them transposed from timber into masonry. In fact, they prove ideally suited here to being wrapped around the tops of circular column shafts in yet a further, mannered incarnation. On the curved walls of the dining room and at the opposite edge of the huge landing, the heavy timber cornices are reduced to decorative elements, "floating" on the upper walls like some Postmodernist gesture decades before Postmodernism was conceived.

A processional hardwood staircase leading to the house's upper storey is interrupted by a narrow landing flanked by an antique ceremonial chair at one end and a cabinet overflowing with dark wine bottles at the other – their aging, ribald labels marking them out as collectors' items. In this space, one has a whiff of the rich labyrinth above: a dwelling unlike any other ancestral house the authors have seen in Iloilo to date.

Even when I was three or four years old, I would go to the house and play. I can say I was Lolo Celso's favourite, as he had no children, and his family was my father's family. That house has so many memories for me as I grew up there. I knew Lolo Celso travelled a lot and he probably got all the ideas for it from somebody he met abroad. We do wonder where all the ideas came from, including that horseshoe table.

Vanessa Ledesma Suatengco, *daughter of Zafiro Jalbuena Ledesma*

We don't really know the history of the house or why Lolo Celso chose these things
for the house. Maybe he was just a collector because he would have lots of cash,
and he would go around the world and collect things.

Patrick Ledesma Jamora, *great-grandson of Celso Ledesma*

After its completion, Celso invited Zafiro, now married to Gilda Laguda and with a growing family, to move into the house – which his nephew dutifully did. Celso continued to travel, tending to his business interests in Negros Occidental and Manila, but stayed in the house while in Iloilo, where he also owned a commercial building, now an iconic heritage structure, on historic Calle Real (officially, J M Basa Street) – once downtown Iloilo's most prestigious business strip. He was to die of natural causes on board a ship en route to Manila.

The house became home to Zafiro and Gilda's children: Celso (his uncle's namesake), who still lives in the house when in Iloilo; Paz, who lives in the US, and her late twin, Hope, who was based in Spain; Gilda, who only recently passed away; Vanessa (now general manager of Manila's 5-star Diamond Hotel); Zafiro II, "Zaffy" – a patron of the arts who would become the popular curator of Museo Iloilo and main custodian of the house until his death in 1990 – and the late Rizal "Dondi", a musician and one of the pioneers of Filipino progressive rock. Neither Zaffy nor Dondi were born when their parents took up residence in the house.

Responsibility for the house now falls on Patrick and his brother Martin, both based in Iloilo. Together with Vanessa, one of the three surviving children of Zafiro and Gilda, and their cousins, they hope that the Celso Ledesma House will one day be registered as a heritage house with its own distinctive plaque.

SIMPLICIO LIZARES MANSION

Talisay City

Baronial Splendour

Standing nobly beneath Talisay's blue skies is a silhouette that perfectly captures the cultivated tastes of its original owners, serving as a prime example of what it must have been like to adapt the most appealing features of Western architecture and design to one's home.

Built in 1930, the Simplicio Lizares Mansion was designed by Juan Nakpil, considered the "Father of Philippine Architecture". Fittingly, it holds a special place in the pantheon of houses that sugar built. While its monumental exterior is more in the Beaux-Arts/Mediterranean style, its interiors lean closer in places to Art Deco. Spanning 3,000 square metres, it was originally meant to be built on a Lizares property on Dewey Boulevard (now Roxas Boulevard), opposite Manila Bay. The Harvard-trained Nakpil scaled back his plans when Simplicio decided to build in Talisay instead.

The Lizares family is considered among the Philippines' true sugar "barons". When Negros was supplying 90 per cent of US sugar imports, a huge chunk of that allocation would have been supplied by the Lizareses, who in the 1930s not only owned numerous *haciendas* but also controlled at least three sugar mills. The family's success is attributed to the business sense inherited from their matriarch, Enrica Alunan Lizares, the legendary "Tana Dicang", who bore 17 children and whose own 19th-century house is now a museum. Simplicio was the eldest boy among 14 children who survived into adulthood. It was only to be expected that he should become a successful sugar planter.

Among his siblings, Simplicio was also the most politicised. In 1934, he was a delegate to the Philippines' first Constitutional Convention and a signatory to the landmark constitution approved by US President Franklin D Roosevelt, which paved the way for the establishment of the Philippine Commonwealth Government in 1935.

"We have a picture of him signing it," says Luci Lizares Yunque, pointing to the framed photograph atop a vintage stereo. Luci, a well-versed spokesperson for the family, is the daughter of Simplicio's son Rodolfo.

The mansion still towers over Talisay. When it was first built, the only other buildings in the vicinity were the

The construction of the house
took a long time as Papa Ande, which
is what we called our grandfather,
kept changing things. This is the only
house with parquet walls that curve
as you climb the stairs. But then if he
didn't like the colour of the hardwood
beneath, he would change it
again and again.

Luci Lizares Yunque, *granddaughter
of Simplicio Lizares*

Church of San Nicolas Tolentino (where Saint Ezekiel Moreno, a Spanish Augustinian Recollect missionary, recuperated from malaria in the 1870s) and the City Hall. Then, the house, in common with several ancestral homes built in Negros and Iloilo in the 1920s and 1930s, was surrounded almost entirely by cane fields. Now the neighbourhood is highly urbanised and commercial.

A few hundred metres from his childhood home, by its conspicuous setting and magnitude, the mansion would serve as an overt symbol of Simplicio Lizares' success as a sugar planter, politician (he served several terms as town mayor), businessman and family patriarch.

With his first wife, Eleuteria Treyes, he sired 11 children – Socorro, Mario (who died in childhood), Rodolfo, Bienvenido Mario, Lucrecia, Simplicio Jr, Amelo, Aurora, Florinda, Eustaquia and Nonata. Eleuteria died in childbirth and Simplicio was married a second time, to Amalia Perez. Simplicio's son Bienvenido Mario Treyes Lizares – who became Mayor of Talisay – would be the last continuous occupant of the house.

The residence's main *sala* recalls in size the drawing rooms of a European palace or English stately home. Luci recalls growing up to much dancing and laughter in this room. The floor is made of panels of native narra, molave

and kamagong wood. Although Art Deco in appearance, the design is pure Lizares.

A full-length portrait of Simplicio and Eleuteria dominates the room. Luigi Lizares Yunque, Luci's son, plans to restore the image. "It was originally a black-and-white photograph that had been blown up and painted over. At first, I thought it was a painting."

The upstairs hallway leads directly to a magnificent smoking room, unique in its day. Two rows of Art Deco club chairs – made, like most of the furniture here, by the House of Puyat – are framed by intricately carved wooden columns. The room's tall, round-headed windows look out over the town plaza from above a narrow *porte-cochère.*

On one side of the hall is the formal wood-panelled dining room, with a table that sits 24 – so long they had to break down a wall to install it. A Second World War bomb is said to have dropped on it; the missile failed to explode and the table survived its weight. The backs of the dining chairs were made to measure, an exact fit for the wall panels.

The floor incorporates motifs that depict the story of the sugar industry. The two *carabaos* [water buffalo] are our beasts of burden. The sun denotes energy, and here is the sugarcane. The "L" monogrammed on these sacks of sugar cane stands for Lizares.

Luci Lizares Yunque

Embedded in the ceiling are wood carvings of assorted tropical fruits. At one end of the dining table, a natty curved Art Deco bar stands against a panel of louvred windows.

Off the hallway, a corridor lit by Czech cut-glass lamps and hung with paintings of the well-travelled Lizares daughters by artist Martino Abellana leads to spacious, interlocking bedrooms. Colour, so dominant in the bedrooms, also marks the mammoth, tiled bathrooms, which are equipped with fixtures – inlaid soap ledges, rounded basins and deep-set baths – familiar to contemporary homes.

The girls' rooms and the master's bedroom are still furnished with their original monogrammed beds, dressers, wardrobes and incidental furniture. The boys' bedrooms, now standing empty, were once located on the ground floor.

Today, the Simplicio Lizares Mansion stands resplendent behind its monogrammed gates, a stately metaphor for a family's enduring respect for the past and the ties that have bound them together through the years. Therein lies the baronial spirit of this remarkable home.

BALAY NI TANA DICANG

Talisay City

A World of Light

This ancestral home is now a museum dedicated to the authentic life and times of the hardworking and prosperous sugar planter, an unmissable stop for those who wish to immerse themselves in the trappings of a gilded age.

Enrica Alunan Lizares is the city of Talisay's legendary Tana Dicang, the diminutive of a title she assimilated from her husband, Efigenio Lizares, who had been the district official known as barrio captain or *kapitan* during the Spanish colonial period (*kapitana* – "tana", for short – being the feminine version of the title).

Little is known about Efigenio besides the fact that Tana Dicang bore him 17 children, but the Lizares family matriarch's influence is evident to this day. It is exemplified by the astonishing grandeur of her home, situated on a quiet side street, and the homes built by her children, including her son Simplicio's magnificent mansion, as well as the preservation of her house as a living museum and art gallery.

As in the nearby Bernardino Jalandoni Museum in Silay, visitors encounter, in the first instance, a historical mode

When the original house was built in 1872, there were no *ventanillas,* everything was closed, and there was no air. But 17 years later, in 1889, Lola Dicang's renovation included the staircase, the four windows and arches. They actually finished the whole house, including the cistern, in 1904. It's all in her notes.

Adrian "Adjie" Lizares, custodian, *great-grandson of "Tana Dicang"*

of transport in the large open space of the ground-floor *silong.* Instead of two-wheeled carriages, however, here it is an *orimon* – a small, shoulder-held form of sedan chair. This would have been used to carry older and more infirm members of the household up the steep, grand timber staircase but also, shaded by an umbrella in high summer, outside on the street.

That staircase certainly seems to have exerted a fascination on the building's occupants: an external set of semicircular steps leads up to the window sill of its low, generous first landing. This was actually an addition during the 1950s, allowing the ladies who lived in the house to enter the driveway in their cars, step out and ascend, via that window, straight upstairs.

The long, thin residence is even set perpendicular to the street – somewhat in the manner of a lavish, extravagantly proportioned coaching house. However, the building's solitary cavernous carriage doorway confirms its true provenance as a family dwelling. With its lower storey of painted or rendered brick (clearly evidenced by a bull-nosed coping course) topped by a timber-panelled upper storey, it is in fact the archetypal house modelled on the masonry-based *bahay na bato* (house of stone), albeit appreciably older than other examples. An information board in the *silong* discloses, "The walls that wrapped the ground floor areas are constructed of stone bound together with an organic mortar and clad on the exterior by rare quarried coral 'coquina' and brick, and covered with lime-wash" – referencing the soft, whitish coquina rock, comprising marine-shell and coral fragments, that was used in a similar way to the seashell lime plaster *chunam,* which gave the British edifices of 19th-century Madras (now Chennai) such a lustrous sheen.

Lola Dicang was very hardworking, domineering and strict. You could only stay in bed if you were sick, but otherwise you had no business lying down. That was her lifestyle. She would give birth and go to work immediately. She had a fleet of wet nurses to care for the children.

Adjie Lizares

Once on the upper storey of Balay Ni Tana Dicang, the timber-panelled enclosure typical of Negros houses takes over – and this time, in great style. Because there were no photographs of the original configuration of the house, its custodian, great-grandson of Tana Dicang, Adrian "Adjie" Lizares, consulted the Escuela Taller de Filipinas Foundation and worked with students at the Carlos Hilado Memorial State University in Talisay to create measured drawings showing how the building had evolved architecturally. Findings indicate three different architectural styles, with the *ventanilla* (lower-window) balustrades providing a clue – the earliest style is more refined, dating to 1889. Later styles are most likely Neoclassical, including those of the *calados* in the *sala mayor*.

While the enormous, full-depth space is decorated with somewhat heavy panelling in customary 19th-century Classical fashion, the rather plain, aforementioned transom-level *calados* are complemented by huge, square equivalents set into the walls. These unique, Neo-Gothic features contain large circular, almost cartwheel-like devices, and lend the *sala* the feel of a screened palace.

Crucially, the lower wainscoting panels (decorated with plain, fielded oval shields) hinge back to reveal floor-level ventilation panels that are as broad as the upper, window-level ones. The hinged opening allows the full width of the lower panel to be opened up to the prevailing breezes, whereas the more usual sliding panels set in their groves cannot be removed in this way and consequently block some ventilation even when drawn back fully. When the sliding screens are also pulled back, the transformation is complete and the openness achieved is stunning – a world of light enters the previously heavy, almost Victorian, upper storey of the house.

Opened to the public in 2008, the museum is also curated by Adjie, a sugar planter and art patron. The grandson of Encarnacion, one of Tana Dicang's six daughters who inherited the house, Adjie grew up here, spending time in the company of his older, widowed grand-aunts after they had moved back. Despite a simple diet of mostly fish and vegetables, his grandmother taught him how to cook pizza and bought him *Time-Life* cook books from around the world, even hiring a chef when he complained he could only eat so much *paksiw* (a dish of fish cooked in vinegar). "I got involved in the house at a very young age," says Adjie, adept at bringing family history to life.

All Tana Dicang's children grew up in the house. Their mother was hardworking and domineering, and intolerant of idleness. After giving birth, she would go to work immediately, leaving her babies to a fleet of wet nurses. The daughters became expert dressmakers in the 1930s – a not-uncommon domestic activity in those

Before evacuating the house
during the war, mother and daughters
inventoried every item in the house.
Each daughter had a copy of the list.
They cleared the house and kept
things everywhere, inside cisterns
and hollowed out bamboo clumps
in the *haciendas*. They knew under
which tree they'd buried the china,
and after the war the daughters were
able to repatriate all her things. The
museum's rule is that family members
can bring things in but they can't
take anything out.

Adjie Lizares

days – sewing fashionable *ternos*, which they themselves
wore fashionably.

Most of the furniture in the house belonged to Tana
Dicang, including the Ah-Tay sets (a renowned Chinese
furniture manufacturer during Philippine colonial times)
in the main *sala*. Hand-painted Kutani tableware from Japan
and pre-1920s crystal high-ball glasses and champagne
saucers attest to a lifestyle entertaining presidents and
members of the Philippine Commonwealth cabinet, the
administrative body that governed the Philippines – barring
Japan's wartime invasion – from 1935 to 1946. Tana Dicang
built a bathroom for the use of President Manuel L Quezon,
who was quite at ease lounging in the main *sala* during
his frequent visits. Nearly a century later, the house still
exudes a sense of soft power.

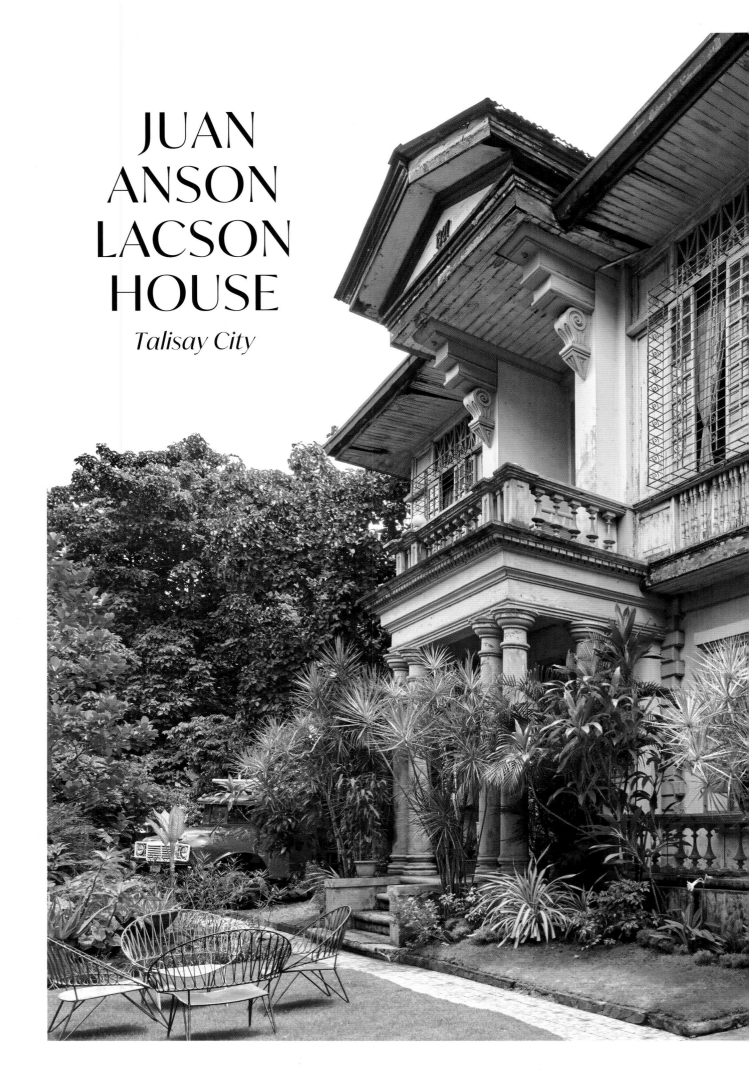

JUAN ANSON LACSON HOUSE

Talisay City

NEGROS OCCIDENTAL ✳

Palladian Pastoral

Tractors, back from the sugar fields, are parked within the relatively small, urban plot on either side of this four-square Classical-style residence in Talisay.

This is one house that deserves the attribution "Palladian" on account of its nominally cubic form, with a narrow, additional wing to the back being marked by a line of rear rustication; Classical detailing; and elevated relationship with its surroundings, mediated through two entrance porches.

The tractors also strike an appropriately bucolic chord; they form a contemporary allusion to the way in which Renaissance master Andrea Palladio built many of his

world-famous residences – in their often-pastoral settings – for the estates of Veneto farmers. In some cases, his clients were so embedded in their rural ways that they even expected to store their grain and other produce in the low but meticulously detailed attic storeys of his country mansions.

All is not strictly Palladian here, however. The smooth, circular columns of the entrance porches (the side one forming an elongated *porte-cochère*) boast a layered version

of the typical Tuscan Order capital, with a further astragal (a small, semicircular moulding) forming a ring "floating" below the standard bulging capital. Dummy pilaster heads divide the side elevations of the house visually into bays without the use of pilasters themselves – an almost Mannerist conceit.

The front entrance porch nestles beneath a dramatically projecting pediment, leading to a large main space – in this case, the *sala*, or living room – in the Palladian manner. However, here, unlike in Palladio's cellular layouts, this hall occupies almost the entire ground floor of the house. Only a partition wall interrupts the spatial flow – and even that was built later to create a bedroom for Felomina ("Lola Mina"), wife of the house's founder, Juan Anson Lacson, when she became too old to climb the imposing wooden staircase with its quarter-turn landing and winders.

The house has been quietly updated through the years. The pale stone tiles on the floor of the *sala* replaced an earlier, darker wooden floor and are even laid in imitation of timber parquet. Elsewhere, a variety of original, patterned tile floors lead one around the large open space, via what

The specific use which Palladio attributes to the "places above" as granaries is confirmed not only by the remarkable roof trusses ... but also by the height at which the window openings are set compared with floor level

Antonio Foscari, *Living with Palladio in the Sixteenth Century*, Zurich: Lars Müller Publishers, 2020, p. 16

[Andrea Palladio's] buildings, particularly his villas, have a flavor never before seen in architecture – a sense of Classical proportion and order combined with warmth and ambiance.

David Jacobs, *Architecture*, New York: Newsweek Books, 1974, p. 124

once was the billiard room (now a dining space) and beneath the upper stair flight.

The forebears of the prolific Lacson family of Negros Occidental originated from Molo, Iloilo – with the progeny of one Domingo Lacson said to have spearheaded the growth of the sugar industry in what entrepreneurial Ilonggos during the 1800s considered "the Promised Land". One of Domingo's sons, Pablo, a prosperous sugar planter, would have nine children, but only one of his four sons would survive. This son, Juan Anson Lacson, was destined to become the father of eight daughters – five from his first wife, Julia Tad-y Jocson, and three from his second wife, Felomina Javier Jimera, who would also give him two sons.

Pablo died early, and the burden fell on Juan, as Pablo's only son, to look after the family's considerable land holdings in Talisay. An older cousin, Esteban Lacson, would help and guide Juan – very much the neophyte and

unaccustomed to the complexities of farming – thereby saving him from exploitation by those all too willing to take advantage of his youth and inexperience.

By the time Juan built his Palladian-style villa in 1927, his elder daughters Elisa, Aurora, Lourdes, Visitacion and Josefa were mostly raising their own families and leading their own lives, and so the house would become the domain of his second family – Fernando, Mercedes, Estrella, Carolina and Ernesto. However, their elder half-siblings would visit often, developing a warm relationship with their stepmother. Bob Diaz Lacson, the son of Fernando, and Julieta "Itang" Yusay Consolacion, the younger daughter of Lourdes, remember the house's convivial atmosphere as well as the trips to Hacienda San Juan, the family farm in Talisay.

Today, the house reflects the beguiling modesty of its current custodian, granddaughter Marina Lacson Go, and

Our families are now many generations old. We need to be able to relay to the generations after us the family stories of what we did and what happened. This includes what went wrong, so that the generations after us do not repeat them.

Larry Diaz Lacson, *grandson of Jose Anson Lacson*

possesses all the charm of a happy home. To the many grandchildren and great-grandchildren of Juan Anson Lacson, the house is their ancestral home. As we have seen, it also manifests a direct connection with the land and the commodity that enabled its construction.

It was Felomina who conceived the unique Lacson tradition that took place annually in the *sala* on the feast of St Joseph, every 19 March. It involved recreating the Holy Family – that is, St Joseph; the Virgin Mary; and the *Santo Niño*, or Baby Jesus – with members of the family handpicked for each role.

The three – typically an older uncle, a teenage granddaughter and pre-pubescent grandson – would then be seated at a round table in the centre of the room, with various aunts coming forward to feed each one. In the background, someone would sing hymns (typically, "Ave Maria"); another would play the piano. The aunts would

take it in turns to wash the actors' hands with perfumed water, after which the spectators – family members and guests – would have to queue to kneel before the "Holy Family", kiss their hands and drop money into a nearby basket. Only when everybody had done so would the ritual be complete, and lunch served. The money in the basket would be divided among the actors.

Says grandson Larry Diaz Lacson, who spent 20 years abroad before returning home to Negros, "This was a family tradition that started when Lola Mina vowed to St Joseph that she would recreate this ritual for the sake of my Dad, who was very frail as a boy. It was to help keep him going. When Lola Mina died, it stopped."

Marina, the daughter of Ernesto, has long since taken over the running of the house, having been adopted by its previous custodian, Tita Mercedes. It is a duty she happily shares with staff who have been with her for over 30 years.

GASTON
ANCESTRAL HOUSE
Manapla

The *Haciendero* Lifestyle

This picturesque mansion with its gleaming white façade and impressive two-storey veranda wears its history lightly.

Set in the middle of Hacienda Santa Rosalia, a 120 hectare sugar plantation in Manapla, in the northeast of Negros Occidental, it was built by Jose "Panggoy" M Gaston between 1932 and 1935 in the colonial-Antillan style. These days, his heirs offer tours and culinary experiences recalling the *haciendero* lifestyle for visitors in search of a bridge to the past.

His son, the 92-year-old secular priest Monsignor Guillermo Maria Gaston (known as "Monsignor GG"), recounts how Panggoy once fended off would-be kidnappers with only a whip, surviving a gunshot wound in the process. Brave, but also hardworking, he put up his home on land inherited by his wife, Consuelo Azcona. Visible from the balcony is the Chapel of the Cartwheels, an extraordinary hut-like structure occupying the plot where the house of Consuelo's parents once stood.

The monsignor says that his father designed the mansion himself, based on his childhood home (now the museum Balay Negrense in the city of Silay) – choosing all the wood and furniture, and envisioning the bathrooms in a similar style but in different colours. He ruled that a painting of the Sacred Heart in the living room should never leave the house, come what may (it is still there to this day). Never known to get angry (his "worst" expression was "Tentacion!"), Panggoy would conduct all business on the ground floor, away from the family quarters upstairs.

Despite his advanced age, Monsignor GG has lost none of his charm or intellectual curiosity. "I love Saint Augustine," he declares, "because he was human. Thomas Aquinas was so cerebral." He strikes one as the perfect priest – comfortingly human yet reassuringly spiritual. The main resident of the plantation house where he was raised as one of eight siblings – Jose Maria, Maria Lourdes,

My mother loved her garden. Of course, she complained about the trees my father planted. He used the end of his cane to dig holes in the ground and secretly scattered seeds. Early in the morning, she was already downstairs taking care of her chickens. Later, she would come up to cook our breakfast. Friends used to say we were spoilt brats because my mother would cook eggs for all eight of us – exactly as we wanted!

Monsignor Guillermo Maria Gaston, *son of the original owner*

Maria Asuncion, Antonio Maria, Victor, Guillermo, Maria Concepcion and Maria Consuelo – he is doted on by his nephews and nieces, many of whom have forged careers in professions outside sugar. The house is filled with family heirlooms, including the antique crystal wineglasses bought by Monsignor GG in Belgium to match his mother's favourite dinner service. A prized possession is the vermillion chalice encrusted with his parents' wedding rings, an idea he copied from Pope John XXIII.

The Gastons trace their ancestry back to a Frenchman from Lisieux, Normandy: one Yves Leopold Germain Gaston. In the early 19th century, Yves travelled to the Philippines to grow sugar and build a sugar mill in Batangas Province as an employee of the industrialist Domingo Roxas. This project may have fallen through, but Yves had found a wife, Prudencia Fernandez, whom he transplanted along with his sugar expertise to Negros. He would make a fortune as one of the pioneers of the sugar industry, working alongside the British diplomat Nicholas Loney. Panggoy was Yves' grandson.

To escape the Japanese during the Second World War, the Gastons fled to safer havens – first to the mountains and later back to Hacienda Santa Rosalia and nearby Silay, then still a town. As it happens, the invaders never seized the house.

Monsignor GG recalls watching dogfights in the sky above the house; to escape stray bullets, the family would sprint across the garden and crouch in a concrete bunker underneath their empty swimming pool. The bunker stood in cruel contrast to a happier hideaway – the siblings'

Our generation knows we need to preserve the house. We each have our duties, what we are capable of doing or would like to do. We all remember so many things about this house, like our grandmother making chocolate out of *carabao's* milk every morning. Everything was created here.

Maria Consuelo Tordesillas Fabregas, *granddaughter of Jose and Consuelo Gaston*

bright-red, concrete playhouse built in the shape of an Elpo brand "rubber shoe", the floor covered with Machuca tiles. Today, the playhouse still exists, a permanent paean to the past.

Such a house was ideal for entertaining, with the dining-room table intended to seat 18. Consuelo would serve her signature punch; the leaves of what appeared to be an ordinary coffee table could be pulled back and folded to reveal a unique mini-bar. The late film director Peque Gallaga, a frequent visitor, was so taken by the house's romantic air (and ebullient parties!) that he resolved to make it the setting of his masterpiece, *Oro, Plata, Mata*. The film's title allegedly comes from an old Filipino custom stipulating that a staircase should not be designed to "end" on *mata* when its rising steps are counted to the chant of "*oro* (gold), *plata* (silver) and *mata* (bad luck)".

At the time, Hacienda Santa Rosalia was my world. There was no other. We grew up enjoying the company of all the farmworkers' children. This little world was big enough for me. Until war broke out, I didn't desire to go anywhere else.

Monsignor GG

The aforementioned Chapel of the Cartwheels is fashioned mainly from discarded materials, including old farm implements – notably, the wheels of carts once drawn by *carabaos*. The repurposed cartwheels surround the chapel, designed in the 1960s by the architect brother-in-law of Monsignor GG, serving as both walls and windows. Even the Christ figure is pinned on a hoisted cartwheel, hardwood slabs forming pews for worshippers below. As an image, it is equally primitive and sublime. Here, every Sunday morning at 10 o'clock, the monsignor would say mass for the local farming community.

Granddaughter Ann Ascalon Soenen – who, by marrying a Frenchman, brought the family full circle – would like the estate to be known for its commitment to the environment and sustainable farming. "My father," adds the noble monsignor, gazing at the windmill set against a blue sky, "was ahead of his time."

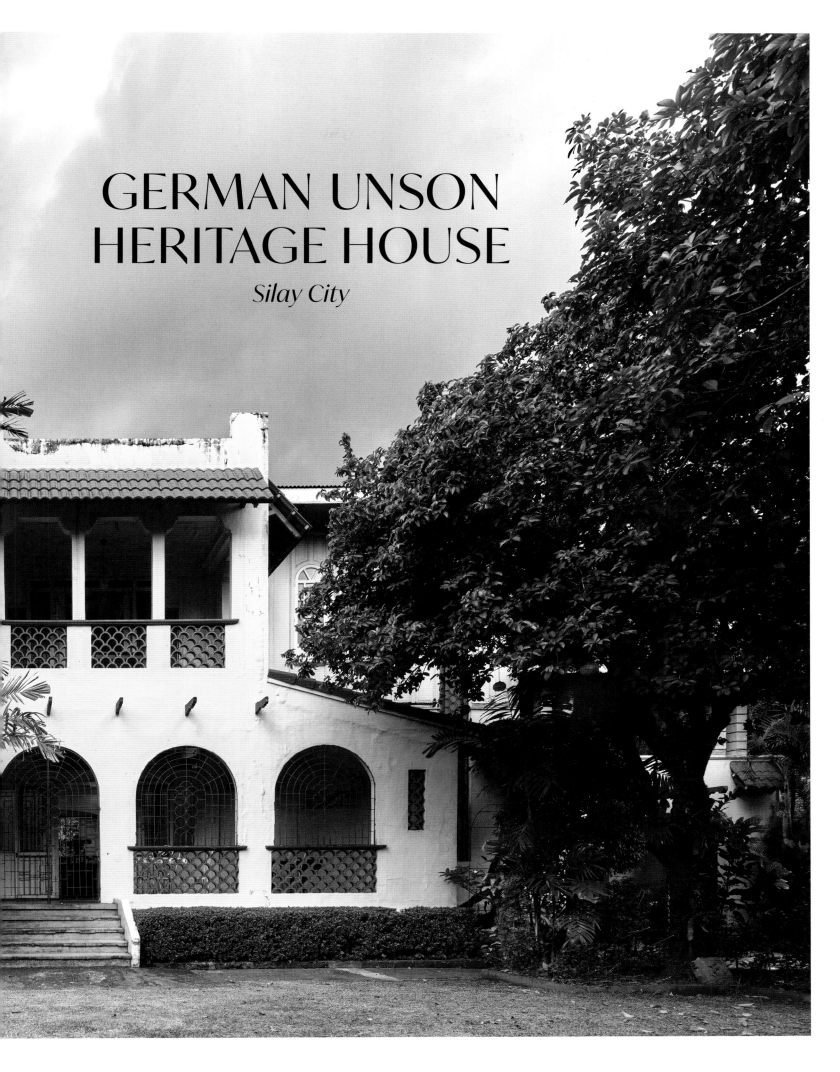

GERMAN UNSON
HERITAGE HOUSE

Silay City

The Soul of a House

Dating from 1938, it may not be as old as other heritage houses in Silay – but the Spanish Colonial Revival home built by German Locsin Unson pioneered, in 2016, the transformation of family mansions in the "Paris of Negros" into charming bed and breakfasts for nostalgic tourists.

Now known as the German Unson Heritage House, it sits astride a manicured lawn on a 2,629 square metre lot. Steps lead from the house's foyer to the long, wood-panelled living room, which can be sealed off if needed by sliding doors. Setting off the cream-coloured panels and anchoring the room are display cases for the family's collection of antique pottery and earthenware. An old harp is propped against a wall, but the room's main feature is a sturdy family heirloom: a 200-year-old spindle cradle used by German Unson's mother, Nieves Locsin Unson, as a baby.

As part of a programme of restoration when the house opened to the public as a B&B, the dining room next to the family room was restored to how it would have looked in 1938. The table and the frames of the dining chairs, with their distinctive rectangular peepholes in the leatherette chair backs, are original, the backs themselves reupholstered.

The heritage house occupies the plot where the timber residence of Dr Lope de la Rama and his French mestiza wife, Carmen Archard, originally stood. Lope was an

eminent physician but according to his great-great-granddaughter and manager of the B&B, the genial Chell Lacson Jimenez ("I belong to the family's fifth generation"), his claim to fame was that as a medical student he was in the same class of 1878 as Dr José Rizal, the revered Philippine national hero, at Manila's University of Santo Tomas. The original admissions certificate bearing both men's names hangs in pride of place in the split-level foyer: a pared-down, light-filled gallery lined with black-and-white portraits of Chell's ancestors.

The house has a romantic, albeit bittersweet, history. While Lope enjoyed prominence as a leader of Silay under Spanish colonial rule, he never remarried after his wife died at the age of 19. Their only daughter, Adelaida, would grow up to marry one Felix Ledesma, member of an equally prominent clan. However, when Adelaida like her mother died young, a victim of typhoid fever, Felix mysteriously vanished – and Adelaida's three children were left in the care of their grandparents, who would make sure they did not want for anything.

Spanish Colonial Revival is as protean in its variability as it is pervasive in its distribution; its presence is ultimately as easy to sense as its characteristics are initially difficult to define.

Reyner Banham, *Los Angeles: The Architecture of Four Ecologies*, Harmondsworth: Allen Lane The Penguin Press, 1971, p. 60

Fe, being the only daughter, was doted on by her Ledesma relatives. Why she should also inherit her maternal grandfather Lope's house when she had two male siblings remains unknown ("Maybe as she was the girl, he felt she had to be looked after," muses Chell).

When Fe de la Rama Ledesma married German Unson, she brought to the marriage the property on which her husband would build the four-bedroom house as it stands today, bearing his name. "This is the reason it is named after my Lolo German," says Chell. Lest there be any doubt, a bust of a smiling, bespectacled German sits on an ornate pedestal by the entrance to the *sala*.

Fe and German's marriage, a true love match, also strengthened the already fruitful ties between two established Silaynon families. German's father, Miguel Yulo Unson, served as Undersecretary of Finance under President Manuel L Quezon in the Philippine Commonwealth Government.

There is a plaque in the family mausoleum with Felix's name,
but his remains aren't there.

Chell Lacson Jimenez, *owner and granddaughter of German Unson*

As was the case for many of his contemporaries – fellow sugar planters – public service was a form of *noblesse oblige*.

An alcove separates two of the house's four bedrooms (the remaining two are on the first floor), all of which have been named after the family members who originally occupied or shared them – German-Fe, Rene, Lourdes and Carmen-Cristina.

The spacious Rene room – actually one of the smaller bedrooms – commemorates the Unsons' only son. Most of the furniture is original, including the hand-carved chairs, tables and lamp stands. The room, which can be accessed from the *sala*, has another door that opens onto an enclosed and gated patio running along the side of the house. From here, one can stroll through a lush garden and pause at the recently built gazebo.

Opposite the Rene room, the master bedroom (German-Fe) retains its original bed and headboard, above which hangs a formal portrait depicting the young Fe dressed in an elegant *baro't saya*, a traditional Philippine costume. Lining the walls of the en-suite bathroom are glass cases filled with Fe's enormous shell collection, a hobby that started with a present from German as she recovered from a broken hip. Perched in the middle of the bathroom is an oval-shaped steeping tub, original to the house.

The staircase, with its original wooden handrail and white-painted wrought-iron balustrades, leads to the open-plan family room, remaining bedrooms and dining room. Nestled in one corner of the landing, an object symbolises by its provenance the family's stature: a grandfather clock

> My grandparents were fond of porches, terraces and balconies, like the one by the stair landing. At one time, we called it the "cactus deck" because it's where my grandmother and aunt used to keep their succulents.
>
> Chell Lacson Jimenez

from La Estrella del Norte, once the largest jewellery store in the Philippines, owned by the Levy brothers. Originating from France, in the late 1800s, the brothers chose Iloilo, the home province of the Unsons, as the site of their first outlet, to benefit from the wealth created by the booming sugar industry.

Up a flight of stairs and on the right wall overlooking the stairwell is an altar filled with religious statues and the devout Fe's personal kneeler. Doors embellished with Art Deco grilles add an air of sophistication to the comfortable family room with its leather sofa, armchairs and photos. Another balcony, this one with a distinctive green-and-red terrazzo floor design, floods the room with light and seems to beckon nature indoors.

If a dwelling does indeed reflect the souls of its inhabitants, the German Unson Heritage House today is distinguished by its heirs' uncomplicated pride in their family history, overlaid with a genuine sense of Ilonggo hospitality.

CASA A GAMBOA

Silay City

A Feast for the Senses

One of the questions confronting the heirs
of families that once prospered from the world's
over-reliance on Philippine sugar is what to
do about their prized possession:
the ancestral home.

D oreen "Reena" Besa Gamboa – owner of Casa A
Gamboa, the characterful house built by her
grandparents – has found her answers.

Not only is she personally overseeing the planting,
harvesting and milling of her family's sugar lands but,
having inherited the sprawling American chalet-style
domicile in Silay (reminiscent of the type identified by critic
Reyner Banham as "California Bungalow"), she is now busy
running it as a bed and breakfast, private dining venue and
event space, with a focus on celebrating Negros' culinary
heritage – a fascinating outcome, given Banham's only
partly tongue-in-cheek "Gourmet Style" follow-up.

Reena is ensuring that Casa A Gamboa – the "A" being the
shared initials of Aguinaldo Severino Gamboa and Alicia
Lucero Gamboa, its original builders – can help to pay for
itself. The house has now become central to the cultural life
of the city, hosting food fairs, shows, exhibitions, weddings
and other events.

Her role model is also the reason the residence now
belongs to her. Doreen Gamboa Fernandez, Reena's aunt,
was a widely revered cultural historian, educator and writer,
credited with raising awareness and understanding of
Filipino food internationally. She died in 2002, bequeathing
her share of the house to Reena, whose passions have
ensured her legacy continues.

Together with Reena's father, Danilo, and sister Della
Gamboa-Besa, Doreen had grown up in their parents' –
Aguinaldo and Alicia's – new house. It was designed and
built in 1939 by the architect Edgardo Lucero, Alicia's
brother, following the strict specifications of Aguinaldo,
who knew exactly what he wanted.

[Of] the two local vernaculars from which modern architecture draws ... the other,
still without a convincing label beyond "California Bungalow" ... is the generalized
idiom ... of low pitched oversailing roofs and wooden walls, open fireplaces and rough
timber, that belongs so much to the restaurant trade in Southern California that it
could carry the soubriquet "Gourmet Ranch-house Style".

Reyner Banham, *Los Angeles: The Architecture of Four Ecologies*, Harmondsworth: Allen Lane The Penguin Press, 1971, p. 73

My grandfather was a practical person. When I was trying to write something about the house, I counted how many doors there were, and I think we have more than 40. There is a room for everything.

Doreen "Reena" Besa Gamboa, *owner of Casa A Gamboa*

Generoso Gamboa Sr ("Lolo Oso"), a sugar planter and agriculturist, had 16 children; Aguinaldo was one of four children by his second wife, Olympia Severino Gamboa (his first wife was her first cousin). Olympia ("Lola Lympia") is written into Philippine history as she and her sisters had sewn the flag raised by Negros revolutionaries, led by sugar planters, to symbolise independence from Spain on 5 November 1898.

Despite, or because of, his lack of interest in academia, Aguinaldo was identified by his father as a future sugar planter. Reena recalls, "Lolo Oso told him not to go to college, but to stay here in Negros and help him with the farm. Which he did, and this is why he somehow became the *padrino*, or head of the family."

All three of Aguinaldo and Alicia's children were raised in the house, which was built after they were born. The siblings loved classical music and jazz; Danilo played the bongos, the girls the piano – with Della partial to Gershwin.

179

Before moving into Casa A Gamboa, Reena first sought the permission of her widowed grandmother, Lola Alicia. Lonely after the death of Aguinaldo, by then she had transferred to Manila, where Doreen and Della were both pursuing careers – leaving the dwelling virtually unoccupied. But by 2019, Reena had realised one of her dreams: to open the house to the public.

At Casa A Gamboa, a wide, granite staircase leads to an elevated porch and two sets of glass-panelled, wooden double doors – one of which opens into the bright living room filled with the work of local artists. To the left is the library, whose focal points are two oversized rattan-fan palm chairs. The house's public spaces – the living room, library and formal dining room – are located on the same floor as the kitchen and bedrooms. Many fixtures and items of furniture, including almost all of the ceiling lamps and camouflaged bar in the living room, are original – ordered directly from a Sears Roebuck catalogue. In the kitchen, which has seen its share of film crews, the flooring, chimney-like oven where her grandmother used to smoke fish, and table are all original.

The narrow corridor leading to the bedrooms is lined in dark-wood wainscoting and mounted cream panels, above which are linear *calados* – a minimal, modern update of

People think that all planters are so rich, but we're all dependent on the farm,
like my Dad was. It was all he knew, and he loved to farm. So if that was taken away,
we would have had nothing.

Doreen "Reena" Besa Gamboa

the ornate pierced transoms installed for ventilation and air circulation in older Philippine homes.

The house's original guest room now accommodates overnight visitors, and contains an antique Chinese trunk returned to the residence by Reena's "Tita" Della Gamboa-Besa, who had found national fame as a concert pianist. In the same room, an Art Deco dresser by the House of Puyat, once the Philippines' most coveted furniture makers, is positioned against the window.

Down the hall, the centrepiece of Doreen and Della's erstwhile room is an intricately carved four-poster bed from the Ah-Tay workshop – with its distinctive rococo headboards, and "calabasa" (squash) and pineapple motifs carved into the rails and posts. The bed in fact used to belong to Reena's great-grandmother, the renowned Lola Lympia.

One recent development that has sparked public interest in Casa A Gamboa is the discovery of proof that General Douglas MacArthur, commander of the Southwest Pacific in the Second World War, visited the house while it was the headquarters of the Fifth American Division. On the day her father died, Reena received an email from archivist Marie Vallejo corroborating what Danilo had long claimed and many local experts ignored – the black-and-white photograph now hangs in Casa A Gamboa's front porch. Months later, Marie followed up with a video of MacArthur's car clearly leaving the Gamboas' driveway.

Casa A Gamboa and a pivot to agri-business has made Reena look to the future with hope, but she is still at heart a farmer: "My uncle says the best fertiliser is the farmer who goes to the farm. So I go, but I don't wear sunglasses and a hat. I have to make everyone feel that this lady means business."

JOSE CORTEZA LOCSIN
HERITAGE HOUSE

Silay City

A Window on the World

If any of the ancestral houses described in this book deserved to be called, quite literally, a family home, then it would be the Jose Corteza Locsin Heritage House in Silay.

Not only was the house's original owner extraordinarily gifted – as a physician, politician and statesman – but, during 46 years of marriage, this quintessential Silaynon "servant leader" and his first wife, Salvacion Montelibano Locsin, begat 17 children – all of whom would eventually live in this "Big House". At 70, Jose remarried and had two more children with his second wife, Delia Ediltrudes Santiago. They too would grow up in the house.

Despite the many accolades, Jose, who served as Governor of Negros Occidental and in the cabinet of President Sergio Osmeña as Secretary of Health, was a modest man – and thus the "Big House", as his family called it, is deceptively simple. Built in the 1930s, it sits on a prominent corner along a quiet suburban street. With its gated mansions and strips of lawn, the area around it is reminiscent of another sugar settlement – Georgetown in Guyana (formerly British Guiana) with its long canals and planted verges.

This residential enclave also, somewhat unexpectedly, brings to mind Helensburgh, the well-to-do suburb that was home to Edwardian Glasgow's shipping and banking tycoons – and, most famously, Walter Blackie, the publishing magnate who commissioned Charles Rennie Mackintosh's world-renowned Hill House.

The Jose Corteza Locsin Heritage House does not hint at Mackintosh-style Art Nouveau, however, but rather an equally unexpected hybrid of Silay sliding-screen residence and the Romanesque. This is because this typical Silaynon house, with its dusty-pink panelling and dramatically oversailing roofs, has been extended to the rear: Dr Locsin wished to add a wing accommodating his surgery and a public entrance where originally a vehicular access ran.

This addition was built in the form of a taller, three-storey block realised in rendered masonry as opposed to the panelling of the main-house wings and bearing the distinctive round-headed arches and "barley-sugar" columns associated with the style known as Romanesque

I helped in the development of the sugar producing industry, from the time of the early stone mill pulled by the *carabao* to the mill run by a huge pot or a wheel that was turned by rushing water and produced *moscobado* [unrefined, muscovado sugar] for the Central [sugar mill] that makes white sugar.

Jose Corteza Locsin, in his autobiography, reproduced in *Substance and Purpose: The Life and Legacy of Jose Corteza Locsin*, Makati City, Philippines: The Urban Partnerships Foundation, 2012, p. 10

When I was young, the *sala* was a forbidden space. Not really forbidden, but you seldom hung out here. In the late 1980s, when it had no real function anymore, it was locked up. When the Locsins would come for Sunday lunch, they used to pass the side of the house, because their elders always told them to preserve this space.

Neil Solomon "Solo" Lopez Locsin, *grandson of Jose Corteza Locsin*

in Continental Europe and Norman in Britain. These twisted columns are called *salomónica* in Spanish, as explained by the *Encyclopædia Britannica*: "**salomónica**, (Spanish: 'Solomon-like') also called **barley-sugar column**, in architecture, a twisted column, so called because, at the Apostle's tomb in Old St. Peter's Basilica in Rome, there were similar columns, which, according to legend, had been imported from the Temple of Solomon in ancient Jerusalem."

They also form a distinctive element of Churrigueresque, the Spanish Baroque style named after the family of 17th-century architect José Benito de Churriguera. Their use here, however, is much more restrained than in this typically florid Iberian idiom – and unadorned, round-headed arches also front the blocky entrance loggia, which, with its plain horizontal parapet, nestles between the oversailing eaves of the house wings on either side.

This restrained approach continues inside, with the wall panels of the large, airy, ground-floor *sala* showing almost featureless detailing and all effort seemingly concentrated on the huge window openings revealed by

that aggregation of small effects ... which is characteristic
of Norman and early Gothic enrichment.

Architecture historian Alec Clifton-Taylor, waxing lyrical about the Norman/Romanesque style in
Another Six English Towns, London: British Broadcasting Corporation, 1984, p. 180

sliding back the multiple shutters. This means that this calm, rational dwelling is remarkable more for the views out offered by this "window on the world" than by ambitious or extravagant internal detailing and fittings. Its main dwelling space, somewhat bypassed by the new entrance, certainly acquired a very particular status.

Proof that this is still very much a family home is evidenced by pictures of the Locsins' large clan preserved in silver-framed photographs dotted around the *sala*. One photo offers a roll call of the Locsin brood: Domingo, Marieta, Lina, Renato, Gloria, Jose, Sergio, Julio, Consuelo, Carolina, Antonio, Isidro, Gregorio, Rafael, Salvacion, Lourdes, Jose III and Maria Milagros.

The walls are also occupied by family portraits painted by prominent artists of the day, such as Felix Gonzales and Pedro Amorsolo, father of National Artist Fernando Amorsolo. But perhaps the most poignant signifier is a

bust by Guillermo Tolentino, on the landing of the classic L-shaped hardwood staircase, of their beloved son Julio Cesar, who died of typhoid at the age of four. So cherished was he, it is said, that his mother, Salvacion, had his remains, at least for a time, mummified. Most of the furniture, from the renowned House of Puyat, is original.

Sadly, the good doctor did not live to see his new surgery put to use; this book-lined room off the raised entrance lobby today has the air of a small library. It also – again, unexpectedly – boasts a quiet tour de force of Jazz Era styling in its striking, circular internal window with tracery comprising multiple Z-shapes and a distinctively Deco, curve-ended shelving unit below.

When his brother's 12 children lost their parents during the 1940s, Jose took them into the "Big House" – a happy arrangement, as the orphans were all their children's double first cousins (Jose's brother was married to Salvacion's sister). Such a large number meant a degree of jostling for space – until the older siblings and cousins moved out.

Silay is still Locsin country. The restoration of one of its newest landmarks, "Balay Puti" (the White House), was a family affair. A 1920s residence, the project was initiated in 2018 by Jose's daughter Lourdes Locsin Buenaventura, and designed by Architect Ed Ledesma of the firm Leandro V. Locsin Partners, with oversight by Solo Locsin. It is now chef Stephen Locsin Escalante's fine-dining restaurant.

One of Jose's orphaned nieces is custodian of the "Big House". Rosario Montelibano Locsin, now in her late 90s, known to all as "Tita Charet", charms visitors with offerings of homemade *dulce gatas*, a sweet made of *carabao* milk and muscovado sugar. "She is the lady of the house," says grandnephew Keeno Lopez Locsin, adding, "This is not a home without her."

HOFILEÑA MUSEUM

1st house in Silay City to be opened to the public, in 1962, 30 years before the next house did likewise.
1st house in Silay, still inhabited, to be declared a museum, in 1990s, by National Commission for Culture & the Arts.
1st house in Silay, still inhabited, to be installed with historical marker, in 1996, by National Historical Commission.
1st successful postwar art promotions & first successful drive for vintage architecture preservation both began here in 1962.
During Marcos presidency, one resident dared oppose & succeeded in thwarting the widening of Silay's highway that would have resulted in the destruction of many ancestral houses & buildings.

HOFILEÑA
ANCESTRAL HOUSE

Silay City

An Artistic Heritage

The extravagantly roofed Manuel Severino Hofileña Ancestral House was built in 1934 by Manuel Severino Hofileña and Gilda Ledesma Hojilla following the birth of Ramon, their second child.

It was the first of the city's many great houses built during the heyday of the sugar industry to open its doors to the public. The Hofileña Museum opened for the first time in 1962, a good 30 years before other heritage houses followed suit, and remains a "must-see" on any visit to Silay.

No one could have been more surprised than Rene Hofileña to hear that his late brother had named him administrator of the Hofileña Museum. Ramon "Mon" Hofileña, who passed away in the summer of 2021 at the age of 87, was in both life and death feted as Silay's "father of heritage conservation". For years, he dazzled visitors, sharing his knowledge and humour while touring them around his family home.

My brother was full of life. He wanted to be involved in everything. As a matter of fact, Mon saved heritage houses in Silay because one day during the 1970s there was a project to widen the roads sanctioned by the government. But he gathered

My two sisters taught piano when there were no auditoriums. During recitals, my father would remove a wall and the stage would be in what was the dining room. The audience would sit in the living room. My other sister would teach ballet, and be allowed to put bars around the room.

Rene Hofileña, *administrator, Hofileña Museum*

the people who were involved in the city's culture and heritage and said, "Okay, demolish our houses, but we will lie in the middle of the road and we are willing to die!" Because of this opposition, the government listened.
- Rene Hojilla Hofileña, *administrator, Hofileña Museum*

The house was built on a row of three Hojilla-owned plots on Cinco de Noviembre Street, within sight of the dome of the city's 1920s Romanesque San Diego Pro-Cathedral, designed by Italian architect Lucio Bernasconi. The middle plot was once occupied by the "mother house" (now destroyed) belonging to Gilda's parents. Its ornate staircase – made of balayong with balustrades carved in Art Nouveau leaf patterns – survived and was bequeathed to Manuel and Gilda. The Art Nouveau-inspired motifs in the couple's new house were designed around this singular, grand stairway.

But who was the architect? Rene Hofileña is unsure – but according to tourism consultant and former Silay Tourism Officer, Ver Pacete, in Silay during this period there were not many formally trained architects. Rather, a *maestro carpintero* – master craftsman – would have built homes like the Hofileñas'. Ver explains that many of these master builders would have been *sakada carpinteros*, migrant workers from China:

We have the longest seaport in Asia here in Silay, and the Chinese would have heard of it. They'd come to Silay, work in the sugarcane fields and when the haciendaros *started to build*

houses, would tell them how in China they had been carpenters or plumbers – and offer their services for a fee.
- Ver Pacete, *tourism consultant*

Most of the Hofileña House's furniture and fittings are original – from the glass panels on the external doors to the round wooden table in what was the original dining room beyond the *sala*. The table still bears the scratches made by Japanese soldiers who commandeered the property during the Second World War.

Since the house was built, this room has been extended to accommodate a long, rectangular dining table and fitted bar. A display case nearby holds a complete dinner service for 24, of German origin. Another cabinet holds some of Mon's precious collectibles: an array of plates, jars, bowls and other vessels unearthed in the Philippines, alongside a 3,000-year-old (Iron Age) Israeli juglet.

The *sala* opens directly onto the Machuca-tiled front portico. The room itself, though not excessively large, is well appointed, with *calados* (pierced transoms) evoking Napoleonic shields. Reassuringly homely, it is furnished with an antique upright piano; ancestral portraits; and a pair of carved, Art Nouveau rocking chairs – a wedding gift to Manuel and Gilda.

The *buena familias* [good families] like the Hofileñas were able to travel to places like Europe and Asia, where they saw the different architectural designs. So when they arrived back in Silay, they looked for a *maestro carpintero* who could have been a painter or landscaper. He would say to them, "Tell me what you have seen in Europe". The *haciendéros* would describe what they had seen, and he would design it.

Ver Pacete, *Tourism Officer of Silay (retired)*

R ene points out that if not for Mon, who for over 40 years also ran the Annual Cultural Tour of Negros Occidental, all the ancestral homes lining Rizal Street, Silay's main thoroughfare, would have disappeared. "Mon is the hero of Negros culture!" he says. "I cannot be compared to him."

The youngest of nine, Rene has a degree in architecture from the University of Santo Tomas in Manila, but spent most of his professional life as a dancer and choreographer. Based in Manila for 24 years, his career allowed him to tour Asia and Europe.

We were spoilt by my parents who allowed us all to pursue our interests in the arts. It all started when as children, they would command us to perform for their visitors, either by singing or dancing. This was a problem because none of us became interested in working on the farm.

- Rene Hojilla Hofileña

While Rene would visit Silay every Christmas, Mon returned from the United States for good after spending years working as a writer, stage actor, and art and fashion model. In Silay, he would re-emerge as an art patron, printmaker and curator of the Hofileña Museum. His portrait as a young

I was so happy to take over from Mon as the house's tour guide, even if in the beginning I didn't know anything about the house. But I was taught everything by our tour guides, and I studied what Mon wrote. Now I have to entertain the guests, and make sure they enjoy. It's like I'm still dancing.

Rene Hojilla Hofileña

man hangs in the house's second-storey gallery.

His spirit prevails. The hallway outside his bedroom – with its four-poster bed, collection of books and DVDs – is a veritable art gallery, every inch of wall taken up by rarely glimpsed paintings by the "rock stars" of Filipino art: Juan Luna, H Ocampo, Felix Resurrection Hidalgo, Juan Luna and Vicente Manansala. In 1974, the house hosted Manansala's one-man show; in 15 minutes, all the pieces had sold. The grateful artist gifted his host several paintings – including one signed to Mon personally.

But perhaps among all the paintings, etchings and sketches, the most poignant is the artwork created by a still relatively unknown Silay artist, Conrado Hudit. "He was completely self-taught. He used to paint cinema posters in the 1960s, but his drawings on black paper and white charcoal were featured in *Reader's Digest*. He died from tuberculosis, penniless." Rene hopes that one day Conrado will receive the recognition he deserves.

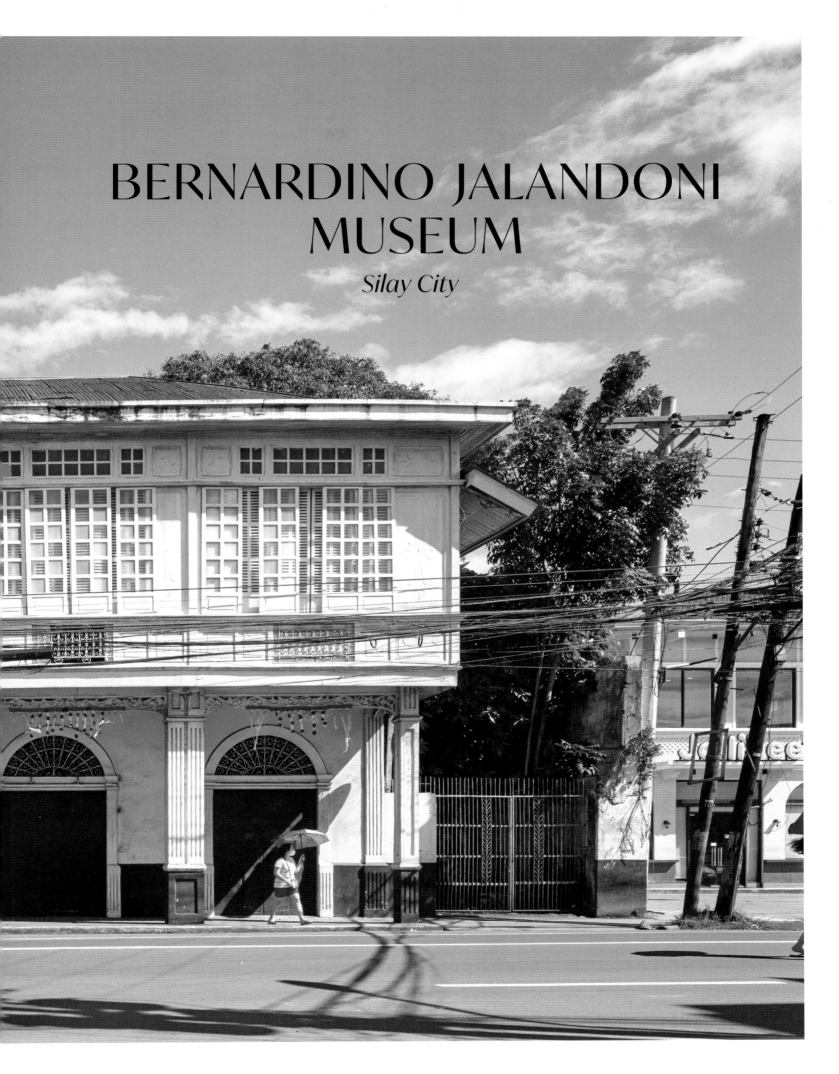

BERNARDINO JALANDONI MUSEUM

Silay City

Remembering our Ancestors

Once a family's urban base, the Bernardino Jalandoni Museum is a time capsule enriching our knowledge of a slice of Philippine history.

It is not difficult to imagine the sumptuous gatherings – akin to European balls of the kind described in *The Leopard,* Prince Guiseppe di Lampedusa's elegiac account of Sicily's 19th-century aristocracy – that might once have been held in the street-front mansion of Bernardino Lopez Jalandoni and his wife, Ysabel Ledesma Jalandoni. A gifted planter and businessman, Bernardino prospered by working on the *haciendas* owned by Ysabel's family at a time of great expansion for Negros Occidental's sugar industry. His

fortune allowed him to buy even more farms and to build this formidable *bahay na bato* house in 1908 along Rizal Street, the main thoroughfare of Silay (once dubbed the "Paris of Negros").

A visitor to the mansion today – as in 1908 – will be confronted in the open ground-floor *silong* by horse carriages and pony traps reminiscent of the Sicilian prince.

At the top of the expressive dark-wood staircase, a charming artefact of bygone days perches on the wall: a

The ground floor or *silong* of the house was not built as living quarters. As with the vernacular *bahay kubo*, the *bahay na bato*'s main living area was raised above the damp earth as it was considered a health hazard ... Rather, the *silong* was intended for storage and as a carriage way. It also served as quarters for the family horse-drawn carriage, the *carroza* ... *and* other heavy religious paraphernalia.

Luca Tettoni and Elizabeth V Reyes, *Philippine Style: Design & Architecture*, Mandaluyong: Anvil Publishing Inc., 2013, p. 18

battery-operated telephone of 1910, of the type normally used by Negros' sugar planters. Its quaint "Rural Line Rules" placard curtly instructs, "When making a telephone call, if the line is not in use, replace the handset on the hook and give *ONE* short ring with the bell crank."

All such quirkiness belies the sheer grandness of the house's first-floor landing space, off which all other rooms open with what can seem a modern, open-plan directness. Like other houses in Silay, the sometimes overwhelming architectural features encountered in fashionable urban Iloilo give way to plain, panelled walls. Here, they are painted a pale mint-green (bordering on celadon), in contrast to the dusty pink of the house's urbane exterior, with greater emphasis being placed on the almost wraparound perimeter sliding screens and panels at both mid and low levels so reminiscent, in intention, of traditional Japanese houses.

Another unifying factor is provided by the huge, rectilinear, carved *calados* transoms, which here occupy panels mimicking the rhythm of the solid wall panels and openings below. As if to emphasise the house's rejection of a

dominant, overarching decorative style, the bedstead in the rear bedroom boasts rather Art Deco cut-out ornamentation in the ambiguous form of either musical string instruments or pineapples – or perhaps a combination of the two?

It was in these surroundings that Bernardino and Ysabel raised their three children – Cesar, Angeles and Juan Delfin – amid furnishings bought in Europe: rows of silver gilt mirrors; Viennese armchairs; opulent dinner services; and musical instruments of the highest order, including a Grotrian-Steinweg upright piano. The ceiling in the main *sala*, which has endured to the present day, is made of embossed sheet-metal panels transported from Germany.

The house was the family's urban base. Typically, *hacienderos* would spend the week on the farm, only returning to their urban residences during the weekends. Eventually, Bernardino and Ysabel moved to Manila and the family of their daughter Angeles, now married to Dr Trino Montinola, became the main occupants of the house with their five children – Isabelita, Antonio, Ester, Luis and Trino.

Among his siblings, it was Tony (short for Antonio), today still sprightly in his ninth decade, who inherited the residence by the quite common practice among old families of casting (and drawing) lots. Tony looks back at the many parties and "jam sessions" that would take place in the house when he was a teenager.

With the encouragement of civic-minded and culturally inclined friends, Tony and his wife, Asuncion "Chona" Sala Montinola, agreed to convert the ancestral home into a living museum; it opened to the public in 1993. Here, family heirlooms and antiques are combined with donations from various sources, including other sugar-planter families – such as a room depicting a typical study, with its vintage roll-top desk and old books, and a bedroom furnished with a four-poster bed that once belonged to the owner of the famous "Ruins" mansion in Talisay. There is also a large wooden ice box, where the family used to store fresh meat. Ice was once a luxury, shipped all the way to the Philippines from Massachusetts, USA.

Tony describes the challenge of restoring and maintaining an old mansion: "The house was swinging and jumping up and down and we wondered why. It turned out that the wooden posts our grandfather had put up were just on ground level. After almost 100 years, the wood had finally broken down. A structural engineer was able to put in a brace so that the house wouldn't fall down. They cut out the bad part of the wood, about 2 feet long, and then

used concrete. We did this for about a dozen posts and so now the house is very stable." The floors, which are original, are made from balayong – native to the Philippines.

When the government considered demolishing some of Silay's historic buildings to build a new highway, the public clamour was such that the idea had to be abandoned. This is evidenced by how the town's main street narrows around the Bernardino Jalandoni Museum, sometimes referred to as "The Pink House", which has remained untouched.

Managed by the Silay Heritage Foundation, the museum does not exist for commercial gain, as both Tony and Chona Montinola make clear. In an interview to mark Negros Season of Culture, 2022, Tony said, "We love the house and want to keep it that way. Not for commercial purposes, as we have more than enough from our farms. God provides the sun and the rain and the funding comes from the Lord". Chona added, "It's truly a great service to the community to have a museum like this. This is also a way of remembering our ancestors and revering their memory. We see them here all the time. We can feel their presence and their guidance, from one generation to the next."

The carriage was crammed: waves of silk, ribs of three crinolines, billowed, clashed, entwined almost to the height of their heads; beneath was a tight press of stockings, girls' silken slippers, the Princess's bronze-colored shoes, the Prince's patent-leather pumps ... They were going to a ball.

Guiseppe di Lampedusa, *Il Gattopardo* (The Leopard), New York: Time Inc, 1960 [1958], p. 215

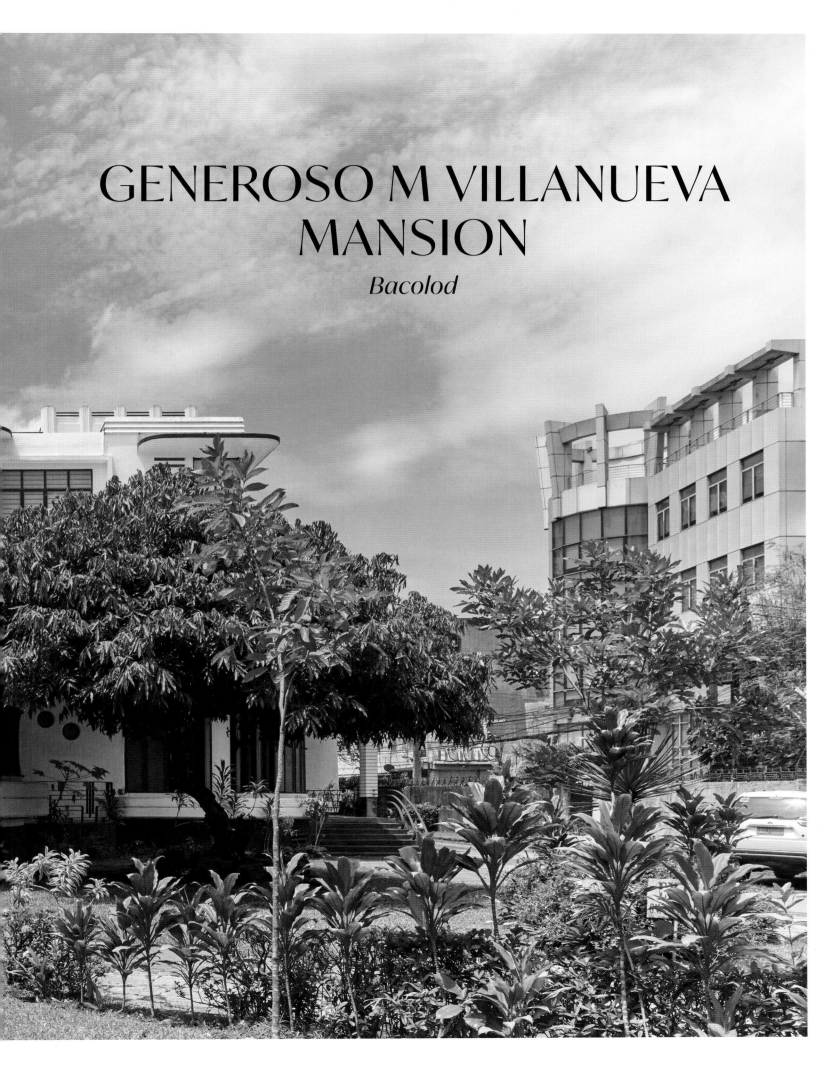

GENEROSO M VILLANUEVA MANSION

Bacolod

"Daku Balay": The Big House

When Lilia Vargas Villanueva first visited New York, her main goal was to see the Art Deco Chrysler Building. Walking excitedly into the lobby of the world-renowned skyscraper, she was overcome by a sense of familiarity: her surroundings looked uncannily like the house of her grandfather Generoso Villanueva, back in the Philippines!

"It's the first thing that came to my mind," recalls Lilia, who has a degree in political science from UC Berkeley. After travelling extensively in Europe and living for over 30 years in Berkeley, California and Tribeca in New York – where she ran an art gallery with her American husband, Craig Scharlin – Lilia returned to her home town of Bacolod in 2012. Today, alongside combining art patronage with property development, she is also the fiercest protector of one of her sugar-planter grandfather's greatest legacies: the massive, streamlined "Moderne" mansion he designed and built in 1930s Bacolod.

Beyond the entrance elevation of the house, with its curving lines and nautical touches, the threshold anticipates the dramatic interiors. A terrazzo floor featuring a pattern of three interlocking rings trimmed with crushed mother-of-pearl shells, rocks and pebbles borders a striped wall ending in thick, concrete pillars framing the narra-wood front door. These pillars are decorated with different earth-coloured bands, suggesting the Italian *scagliola* technique wherein paint is compounded into the cement. It is unclear how Filipino craftsmen of the time would have mastered such a procedure. Had there been an Italian in their or the family's midst to influence them?

On entering the house, one steps into a vestibule offering a direct view of the sweeping, conch-shaped staircase. What used to be a living room to one's left is now an office, but this generous space dotted with concrete pillars hints at a past life of glamorous social events. The floor comprises a selection of Philippine hardwoods including molave and ironwood, arranged in intersecting geometric patterns. However, at the far side of the room is an example of the eclecticism that pervades the residence: cloud fans suddenly appear, exquisitely carved into the floor. This particular feature is said to have endeared the house to the Japanese general who requisitioned it during the Second World

This [balcony] was where everyone retired after the meals to play mahjong or panguingue, as there was a lot of breeze. I really think this would have been an integral part of the house because of all the attention to detail and how everything is so symmetrical. Look at how the porthole on that wall corresponds to the porthole on the opposite wall.

Lilia Vargas Villanueva

War; he repeatedly assured the family that it would not be destroyed afterwards.

The erstwhile dining room leads to a spectacular half-moon balcony with unique flourishes such as the tiny half-moons painted onto its colourful terrazzo floor at the base of twin columns and a fantastically painted ceiling.

According to Lilia, although Generoso Villanueva inherited sugar lands from his father, Basiliso, he was largely self-made. By the time her "Lolo Gener" moved his beautiful wife, Paz Gonzaga Villanueva, into the house in 1936, he was already a powerful figure and major player in Negros' burgeoning sugar industry. Lilia recounts the oft-repeated family story about her grandfather wanting to build the tallest building in the city so that he could

look down on those who had belittled him as he worked his way up.

True to his word, what the family has always called "Daku Balay" (Big House) was the tallest building in Bacolod until 1959. It also boasted the city's first domestic elevator: doors embedded with glass portholes hand-painted by Generoso's niece Lucy Villanueva (evoking everything from Philippine pastoral scenes to Matisse's dancers), the elevator would transport guests from the ground to the first floor. They stepped out of a small alcove onto a well-lit roof deck especially made for dancing – complete with sunken musicians' pit.

Lilia, whose father, Oscar, lived in the house along with his four siblings – Alicia, Mario, Virginia and Generoso Jr – says that the house was meant for entertaining. But it

Automobiles, airplanes and ocean liners, all regarded as sleek, futuristic shapes, are symbols of utmost technological advancement of that particular modern age, causing this 1930s off shoot of art deco to be called the "moderne" style

Augusto F Villalón, "Peeling Away Layers of Ilonggo Architecture", in A Feleo (ed.), *Iloilo: A Rich and Noble Land*, Metro Manila: Lopez Group Foundation, 2007, p. 105

was also clearly a canvas for her grandfather's creativity. No evidence exists that the family patriarch ever left the Philippines, but his frequent travels to Manila (where he owned a house) meant he would have been inspired by the international mixture of Art Deco, Art Nouveau and Bauhaus styles that local architects such as Andrés Luna de San Pedro were introducing into Philippine urban and domestic architecture during the American colonial period. Thus, when it came to creating his own home, the senior Generoso had only to tell his engineer, Salvador Cinco, what he wanted. Skilled workers from the Philippine provinces of Nueva Ecija, Romblon and Sorsogon were lured to Bacolod and housed behind the building site – along with their families, if necessary.

The second storey, assigned to the daughters, opens up to walls wrapped in a plaster bas-relief mural depicting Generoso's life. To the left of the stairs is another floor-to-ceiling bas-relief, depicting the leaves of a coconut tree.

At the centre of the first-floor hallway, a hole let into the floor is surrounded by an oblong cast-iron balcony replete with portholes patterned after a ship's hull. Lilia remembers,

I have learned this is really my grandfather's story. [In the mural] he depicted the farmers as strong, with Graeco-Roman women symbolising abundance, as he also had a three-hectare fruit orchard. Fanciful animals because he loved them, and a *haranista* [serenader] since he loved music. There is a *bahay kubo* [traditional timber-and-thatch house on stilts], a sugar mill and the Philippine sunset. So you see this is a very modern house infused with traditional Philippine symbols. It's a reminder of who he was, a Filipino.

Lilia Vargas Villanueva

"We, the little ones, weren't allowed to attend the adults' parties, but we would crouch down here and see who was arriving, comment on what they were wearing and watch the dancing."

Lilia's favourite room in Daku Balay was arguably also her grandfather's. Located on the top floor, the breathtaking Spider Room – once Generoso's recreation room – takes its name from a peculiar ceiling detail: a web attached to a golden metal spider and fly. This is also where Generoso's love of animals would have found its true expression – with walls transformed into murals of monkeys clambering over branches and swinging on trees, and terrazzo flooring inlaid with other animal figures such as frogs, *carabaos* and snakes. A serpentine predisposition is, in fact, manifested elsewhere in the Big House – most notably, in the two snake heads carved into the rear entrance. "I also have a love for animals," says Lilia, "so this aspect of my grandfather brings me closer to him. I know I can restore his house." And with it, a beautiful work of art.

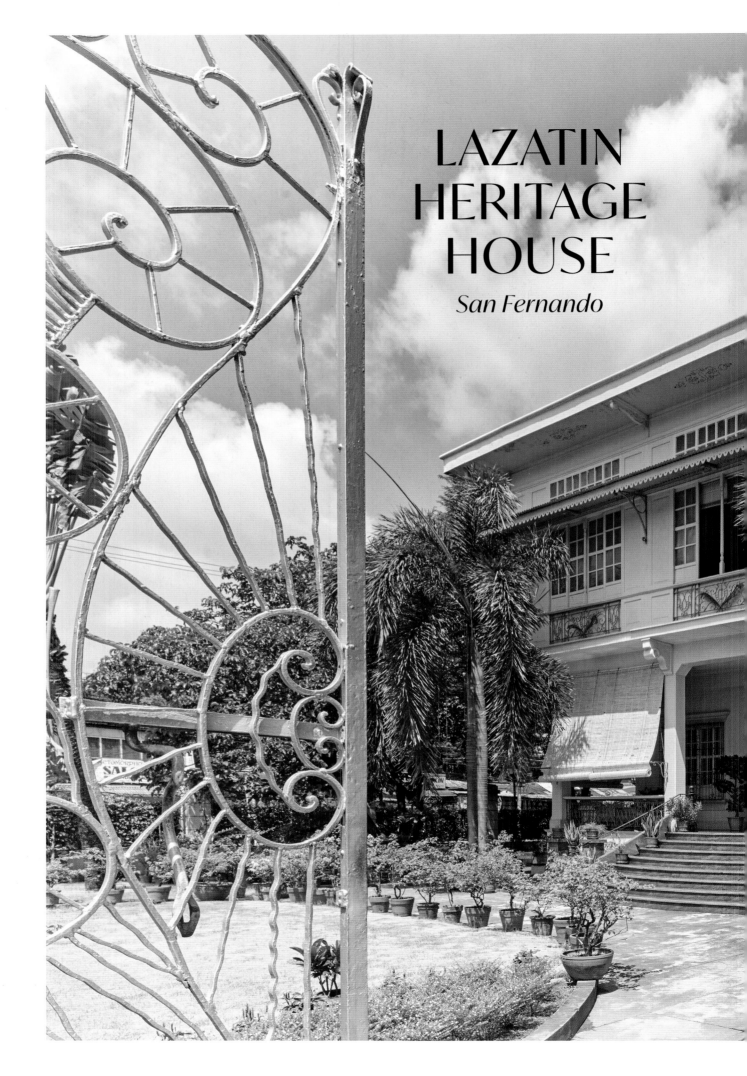

LAZATIN
HERITAGE
HOUSE

San Fernando

A Neocolonial Tour de Force

Behind florid wrought-iron gates stands a mansion symbolising both the refined sensibilities and the prowess of the family that built it.

Today, the descendants of Serafin Ocampo Lazatin and his wife, Encarnacion Torres Singian, continue to nurture their ancestral home in the city of San Fernando, Pampanga's bustling capital. They manage to keep this 1926 Neocolonial masterpiece, with its generous portico and languidly billowing blinds reminiscent of a Southern American plantation mansion, seeming at once pristine and lived in.

The house bears the fruit of successful restoration,

maintenance and investment through the years, and is thus a harmonious blend of the old and the relatively new. A Machuca-tiled porch leads to a front door stripped of white paint to reveal its original varnish – a task accomplished only after the unmarried daughters, Anita and Carmen, the last Lazatins to reside in the house full-time, had passed away.

Upon entering the front door, one steps immediately into a formal, refined living room and reception space. The living room is furnished with a sofa and armchairs acquired in the 1980s to replace the original fittings. Earlier, in the 1970s, the family had installed a wooden, ceremonial archway between the living room and dining room – a product of the superior wood craftsmanship found in nearby Betis, one of Pampanga's oldest districts.

The hardwood floors are original; however, the debossed timber-panelled walls, specifically those in the dining room, are relatively new, as Marco Lazatin – the youngest

We changed the walls in the 1980s because they were only made of narra plywood.
Even that wasn't original, as when they finished stripping the plywood, they
discovered walls with a hand-painted bamboo leaf design underneath.

Marco Lazatin, grandson of house builders Serafin Ocampo Lazatin and Encarnacion Torres Singian

of Serafin and Encarnacion's 19 grandchildren, and the
house's designated custodian – explains above.

The L-shaped staircase leading to the family's private
quarters is original; for fun, Marco and his siblings
used to slide down the steps on their backsides. At
the top of the stairs, wooden double doors open to reveal
a long, narrow hallway and gallery adorned with family
portraits and a framed photograph of Encarnacion's
brother, Dr Gregorio Singian, the first Filipino surgeon.
Doors open to a series of luxuriously appointed bedrooms,
their entrances softened by *portieres*, or door curtains. At
one end of the hall, four armchairs with ornate backrests
surround a table – intimating a cosy, elegant parlour.
    Marco also acts as curator of the many family heirlooms
and artefacts accumulated by Serafin, Encarnacion and their
eight children: Cristino, Maria Ester, Remedios, Corazon,
Anita, Consuelo, Jesus and Carmen. These range from the

When my grandparents first built the house, this was the suburbs. There were no houses past this. This was the edge of town.

Marco Lazatin

matriarch's enviable toy collection to the bookcases stuffed with first editions in their original dust jackets, to a unique assemblage of matchbooks displayed on a bedroom wall and oil paintings by his Tita Carmen, who took up painting at the ripe old age of 82. There are also the silver *paliteras*, ornate silver toothpick holders de rigueur in affluent family homes in the 1800s.

His grandfather Serafin enjoyed a good head start in life. Marco recalls an aunt telling him that his great-grandfather Esteban Lazatin recognised Serafin, his youngest son, as the one who would work hard on the land and make something of it – and thus leased to him some of his best properties. Serafin became not only a successful sugar planter but also a surefooted businessman. He was the first president of the San Fernando Electric Light and Power Company, the city's energy supplier. Fifty-one per cent of SFELAPCO was owned by the Pampanga Sugar Development Company (Pasudeco), founded by Serafin and other prominent sugar planters in collaboration with a group of American investors in

1918. Future generations of Lazatins would turn out to be equally entrepreneurial, setting up San Fernando's first supermarket, Essel (a reference to the names "Encarnacion" and "Serafin").

Marco never met his grandfather, who died in 1951, but remembers his grandmother and maiden aunts occupying a bedroom off the ground-floor dining room. The house was under the care of his aunts until Carmen passed away in 2010. Before she died, she requested that she be moved to a room upstairs with a four-poster bed, and the family carefully converted a suite of rooms for her use – even adapting a bathroom with the most up-to-date facilities to accommodate her infirmities.

Sisters Carmen and Anita were the ones responsible for setting up Essel. Their hard work and devotion led to the business influencing domestic lives (they introduced household items previously unknown to San Fernando shoppers) and food tastes (they introduced *jamon serrano* – dry-cured ham – in the 1970s and croissants in the in-house bakery).

However, to the benefit of their home, they also travelled extensively for leisure, visiting Europe and bringing back pieces of furniture that still adorn the bedrooms – including an inlaid wood headboard and side tables from Sorrento – as well as decorative plates and religious icons commemorating their trips. A bathtub carved out of one solid piece of marble lends an air of glamour and sophistication to an upstairs bathroom. In the spirit of adapting to the times, the ceilings in the bedrooms upstairs were lowered in the 1970s when air-conditioning was installed.

Jai alai, which literally means "happy feast" in Euskara and is the name of a variant of Basque *pelota*, was for a long time a popular betting game in the Philippines.

Marciano R. de Borja, *Basques in the Philippines*, Reno, NV: University of Nevada Press, 2005, p. xv

During the Japanese occupation, many great houses were requisitioned as headquarters – and the Lazatins were forced to flee their home for Manila, having heard of the atrocities being committed by the invaders. The house was taken over by General Masaharu Homma, the Supreme Commander of the Japanese Imperial Army; fortunately, it was left largely intact.

A first-floor veranda overlooks a *kamalig* (a form of *bahay kubo*, or *nipa*-clad hut) on the house's grounds, originally meant to store grain and rice. In the 1970s, this was converted into a *pelota* court, a small example of the continuing Basque influence in the Philippines.

However, as the family grew, and the dining table in the house could no longer accommodate everybody, the structure was made into a generous entertainment space fit for a clan.

233

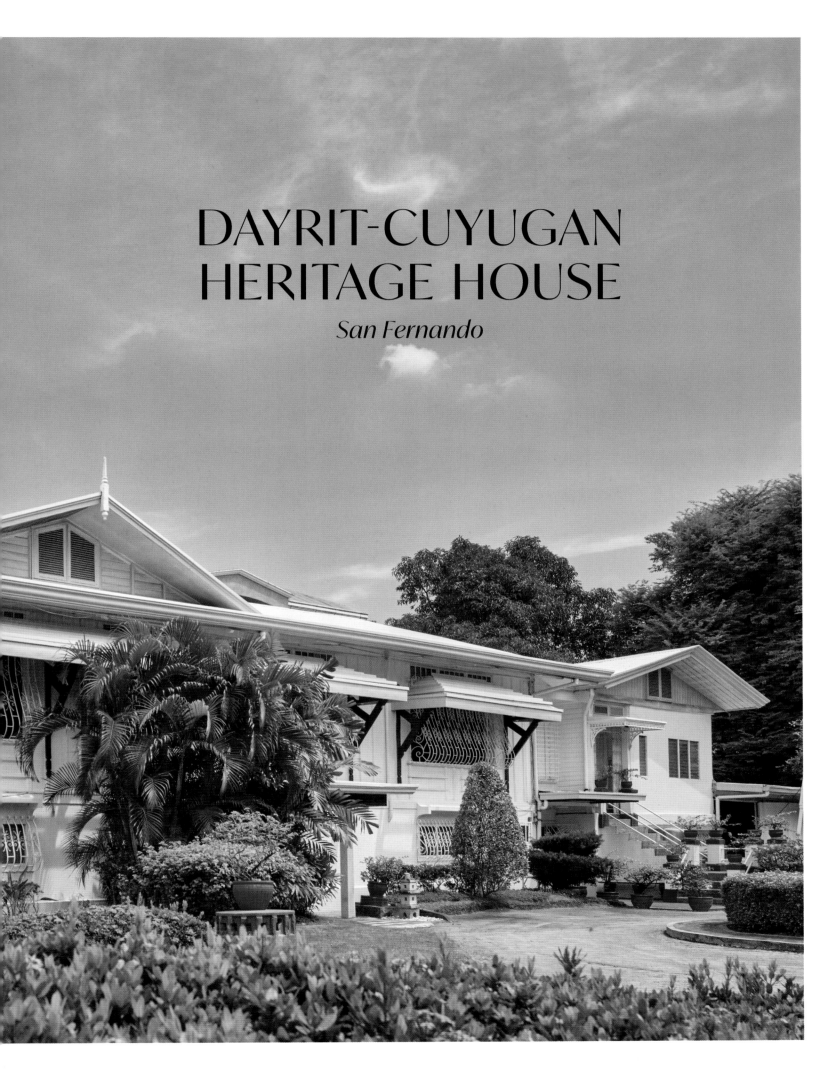

DAYRIT-CUYUGAN
HERITAGE HOUSE
San Fernando

The "White House"

One of the most visible landmark dwellings in San Fernando, Pampanga, the historic Dayrit-Cuyugan House is the ancestral home of an old, traditional Kapampangan family whose current owners have been quietly and studiously preserving its legacy for the next generation.

The people of Pampanga call it the "White House". This American Colonial residence with its immaculate façade and dramatic overhanging roof, reminiscent of the roofscapes of Frank Lloyd Wright's Prairie Houses in the United States, is clearly visible on the San Fernando side of the busy MacArthur Highway – the second-longest road in the Philippines. But to get a little closer, one has to pass through Art Deco iron gates and cross a generous driveway.

When Joaquin Singian Dayrit of San Fernando took over the property owned by the family of his first wife, Paz Cuyugan, it was not much more than a traditional Philippine *nipa* hut. However, by 1920, with the help of a master craftsman, Joaquin, a sugar farmer, had gone on to build what was destined to become a genuine Pampanga landmark, owned and still lived in by his direct descendants. The family refers to their inheritance as "Bale Maragul", another version of "the Big House". They insist that it is not, as is often claimed, a *bahay na bato* – and, indeed, the prevailing American Colonial treatment, with timber clapboard walls and generous veranda spaces, would seem to confirm this.

Joaquin and Paz had 10 children, of which eight survived to adulthood: Luz, Emilio, Virginia, Godofredo, Honorio, Romeo, Natividad and Eduardo. Joaquin was a big man; his uniform was white *camisa chinos:* collarless, cuff-less T-shirts said to have been adopted from the Chinese. A forceful character, he had a big, booming voice. His favourite expression was "Punyemas!" ("How irritating!") – and he liked to throw parties, at which local and national politicians were frequent guests.

In 1972, his eldest daughter, Luz Dayrit-Rodriguez, who in 1941 married Ulderico Rodriguez of Bacolor (a *haciendero* like her father), bought the house from her siblings, undertaking considerable restorations before moving in permanently the following year with their four children

– Elsie, Edgardo, Evelyn and Edwina. Except for Edwina, known as Winnie, the siblings all reside in the house.

One imagines how, before the influx of vehicular traffic, entering the Dayrit-Cuyugan House would have been possible from the main road via the perron staircase leading to a wide veranda laid with Machuca tiles. One section of the otherwise well-preserved floor has been permanently defaced by a missed bullet meant, many years ago, for one of Joaquin's sons.

Two sets of glazed wooden double doors with original Art Deco-style grilles and separated by a panelled wall provide symmetry, beckoning visitors into a spacious and light-filled formal *sala*. Complementing the hardwood floors are furniture by native Kapampangan craftsmen. These form a neatly arranged combination of antique planter's chairs, high-backed wooden sofas, side tables inlaid with mother-of-pearl, and similarly inlaid *solihiya* (described as "rattan strips woven into sunburst patterns") armchairs with wooden cartwheel armrests. The "pregnant", wrought-iron *barrigon* window grilles are a 1970s addition. The beautiful antique, drip glass chandelier once graced another ancestral home, related to the family, from the nearby town of Mexico.

The climate being what it was ... I gave broad protecting roof-shelter to the whole,
getting back to the original purpose for which the cornice was designed. The underside
of the roof-projections was flat and light in color to create a glow of reflected light ...

Frank Lloyd Wright, explaining the rationale behind his famous "Prairie Houses": Frank Lloyd Wright, *An Autobiography*, 1932

This isn't only the house that sugar built but also what "gambling" built. Because my grandfather had Monte downstairs in our kitchen. Monte is a card game. There was a banker from Manila who would come here. A lot of prominent people would come to gamble in the afternoon.

Evelyn Rodriguez Candelaria, *granddaughter of Joaquin Singian Dayrit*

The renovated lower floor, accessible by an indoor staircase, was once used by Joaquin as a gambling den, where men of means (some more than others) would gather every day to play "monte", the Spanish card game similar to basset. Both Evelyn and Edwina recall coming in every day to eat *arroz caldo*, a type of congee served to the gamblers for the price of 20 centavos. The children would leave the house clutching one peso each, a princely sum from their Lolo Joaquin. When their mother, Luz, bought the house from her siblings, she had the entire space renovated into low-ceilinged bedrooms.

Beyond the *sala*, a three-quarter built-in wall divider was added during the 1970s restoration to separate the dining room from the staircase and the living room. Between the dining room and kitchen is a butler's pantry or scullery that today contains a vast collection of kitchen gadgets, attesting to the high status that Kapampangans attach to food and the culinary arts.

In the past, the upper floor used to contain all the living quarters, including the bedrooms. However, the first door to the left as one enters the living room once accessed the prayer room, which still harbours near life-size statues of the ivory-faced Our Lady of Sorrows and Saint Monica that used to form part of the annual Lenten procession.

When Joaquin remarried following Paz's death, his new wife, Trinidad Canlas, is said to have refused to live in the house, and the couple built a new residence across the road.

As the de facto matriarch of the family, Luz Dayrit-Rodriguez proved to be a hard worker. She inherited much of her diligence from her mother, who used to have a fleet of *calesas* (horse-drawn carriages) plying the route from San Fernando to the town of Arayat and back, transporting goods. She was also known as both a gourmand and

Our mother was more of a worker than we are. She was a pharmacist and graduated from Centro Escolar *magna cum laude*. She also had a drugstore in downtown San Fernando called Farmacia de San Fernando. After my father got sick, she was the one who took over the farm. There was no one else to take over, and we were still at school.

Evelyn Rodriguez Candelaria

gourmet cook, her speciality being a now-rare pork known as *cabeza de jabali*. At family gatherings, her finely dressed table would be laden with *lechon* (suckling pig), turkey and *lengua* (beef tongue).

Financially conservative, if not completely frugal, her children would remember Luz advising them to be careful with money; she would claim that the family was in serious debt. Only later did they realise that what Luz was referring to as debt were agricultural crop loans renewed on an annual basis. In which case, almost every sugar-farming family would be equally in debt.

The Rodriguez siblings are aware that their next generation only consists of two – Evelyn's daughter Jacqueline Anne Rodriguez Candelaria, a Manila-based banker, and Winnie's son Rafael Rodriguez Ramirez, who like his mother is based in Vancouver. Indeed, in the medium to long term, the fate of the Dayrit-Cuyugan

ancestral house pivots on the decisions this, the third generation, make on where they choose to live and how they spend their lives.

FROM TRADE WINDS TO TRANSOMS

The Houses that Sugar Built: An Architectural Overview

As the visitor steps out onto the Classical elevated portico of the **Juan Anson Lacson House** in Talisay in the Philippine province of Negros Occidental, they certainly experience the "sense of devotion and majesty" to which Andrea Palladio refers in this extract from his famous *Four Books on Architecture*. The Renaissance Master was well known for his designs for the mansions of Venice's "republican men of affairs",[1] and the commercial "aristocracy" of Italy's northeastern Veneto region for whom Palladio designed his lavish residences might serve as a model for the planters who erected the magnificent houses of 19th- and 20th-century Iloilo, Negros Occidental and Pampanga. One particular product – sugar – contributed significantly to the wealth of these provinces, making these lavish residences examples of what we might call "commodity houses". A similar phenomenon can be seen in instances as diverse as the UNESCO-listed city of Cienfuegos in Cuba, with its connections to the island's burgeoning sugar industry and its unrivalled ensemble of 19th-century Caribbean Neoclassical structures, and the 18th-century *landhuis* mansions of Batavia (now Jakarta) in a Java overseen by the Dutch East India Company's "coffee sergeants",[2] on which rested the Indonesian trading city's self-styled architectural reputation as "Queen of the East".

Despite the overwhelming influence of the "commodity" aspect (hence, the title of this book), such grand residences in a nation with a history of colonial occupation also highlight a second issue: whether or not they represent an attempt to forge a national style. Efforts of this kind can be witnessed in some nation states emerging from colonialism, as in the tenacious but ultimately frustrated attempts of Hassan Fathy to define a national architecture for the New Egypt. However, they are emphatically absent in others: witness, still within the African continent, the eclectic diversity of built work that characterised newly independent Morocco or Mozambique[3] – and, indeed, the heady variety of the Philippine mansions, which (as the house descriptions in this book recount) often combine multiple "layers" of remarkable stylistic blendings. In the Philippines, this picture is complicated by two different phases of colonial rule: by Spain, from 1565 to 1898, and the United States (1898–1946, with a short hiatus during the Japanese occupation in the Second World War), both of which have left their mark on the islands' architectural heritage.

A final subject for this architectural overview concerns the relevance of a vernacular regional prototype for these houses. While the postcolonial Philippines does not seem to have embraced a national style, even the grandest mansions of Iloilo and Negros featured here appear to harbour some memory of the islands' much-lauded *bahay kubo* (square house on stilts). Furthermore, despite the archipelago's great geographical and cultural diversity, they exhibit these traces in a way that echoes the experience of smaller and more homogeneous ex-colonial nations. Here, we might note the Portuguese- and Dutch-inflected residences of Geoffrey Bawa, which did so much to forge a postcolonial style for Sri Lanka, in contrast to the experience of larger, more diverse territories like neighbouring India.

These three routes into the architectural background of these remarkable houses could be seen as investigating, respectively, their international, national and regional/local aspects. Such an approach takes the form of a focusing down from the economic/urban aspects of these settlements to the stylistic and detailed elements of their individual monuments – one might say, from trade winds to transoms.

245

Clockwise from left: **"The Ruins"** (early 1900s) and **Simplicio Lizares Mansion** (1930), both in Talisay; **Celso Ledesma House**, Iloilo (1922); **medieval merchants' houses** cheek-by-jowl with the **Holsten Tor gatehouse**, Lübeck, Germany; **Guildhall**, Lavenham, Suffolk, England.

Commodity Houses

The recollections of merchant Lin Wei-sung – recounted in Nora Waln's memoir of 1920s China, *The House of Exile* – testify to the extent of global trade before the arrival of European powers like Spain, which established the "Galleon Trade" bringing exotic goods from China through the Philippines to Acapulco on Mexico's Pacific coast.

Within this commercial setting, no trade was more important to the Philippines itself than that in sugar. A history of the Victorias Milling Company, based in the province of Negros Occidental, recounts that (perhaps in more ways than one), "[i]n the Philippines, running short of sugar is taken as badly as running short of rice".[4] The industry was, in fact, still luring Chinese workers into the 20th century – and the chapter here on the **Hofileña Ancestral House** in Silay describes how these resourceful migrants transitioned back from field labourers to the skilled building craftspeople they had previously been (the so-called *sakada carpinteros*).

Such trade brought wealth, from which ever-grander houses could be built. As architectural historian Bill Risebero notes, great building periods are underpinned by economic developments and (often new) sources of wealth.[5]

Pre-modern Examples

The typical brick medieval merchant houses of Dutch trading towns and their eventual competitors, the German Hanseatic "free cities" such as Lübeck and Hamburg, testify to a regional trade that helped lay the foundations of modern seaborne commerce. The diminutive Vietnamese port of Hoi An, however, speaks of an exchange closer in nature to those described between the precolonial Philippines and China, above. From the 15th century onwards, the monsoon-driven trade winds brought merchants from China and Japan in the north, and Indianised Southeast Asia to the south and west, to Vietnam's central coast. Being obliged to wait for the return-wind season, they built houses there – gifting Hoi An a unique heritage of Chinese-, Japanese- and Indo-Chinese-style dwellings alongside traditional Vietnamese models.

In some cases, a single commodity comes to dominate: silver, for example, in the 13th-century central Bohemian "boom town" of Kutná Hora (source of the Prague *groschen*, a Euro-style currency once accepted throughout central Europe) or textiles in the medieval "wool towns" of Suffolk and Essex in eastern England. Such examples display the tight-knit urban pattern of a period before mass communications and imperial trade. Lübeck's 13th-century

Through history we traded amicably with the Philippinos. When Western ships sailed into Manila, the major population was Chinese. The commander of these stranger ships said that his birthplace was called Spain.

Lin Wei-sung, Elder of Hopei Province, China, quoted in Nora Waln, *The House of Exile*, Harmondsworth: Penguin Books Ltd, 1938, p. 14

merchant houses not only crowd closely together, they also sit hard by the Holsten Tor – the urban gatehouse that served as a storage depot for Baltic salt in the city's trade with Scandinavia and Russia. Medieval Lavenham in Suffolk grew unprecedentedly rich from the wool trade with the Low Countries and France. With its iconic timber-framed houses, the town's urban morphology culminates in the enormous Guildhall, which dominates the main square but is still essentially residential in form. Such a pattern can equally be a springboard to opulence: many of the guild houses at the other end of this textile trade, in Flanders (northern Belgium), show a decorative exuberance that would put prudent Lavenham to shame.

Such individual expression is evident in Philippine residences like the **Generoso M Villanueva Mansion** in Bacolod City, whose builder is said to have wished to erect the tallest house in the city so that he could look down on all the people whom he thought had once belittled him. It points to the spacious layouts of these houses and to a later era – one that includes the Rhode Island mansions of Richard Morris Hunt for the steel and banking tycoons (rather than commodity barons) of an expanding and confident United States, and the relaxed arrangements of William Hesketh Lever's Port Sunlight in northwest England. They also share an extravagance that marks these examples.[6]

The Modern Era
In late 18th-century Britain, Bristol's iconic Georgian House (home of sugar merchant John Pinney, who had plantations on the Caribbean island of Nevis) and the sober mansions of Glasgow's "Tobacco Lords" (grown rich on imports from the plantations of Virginia in North America) lie on the cusp of this change. They embraced the supremely adaptable Neoclassical style, perhaps best epitomised in the British Isles in the New Town development of Glasgow's great Scottish rival, Edinburgh.

Although the Philippines houses belong, as we have seen, to a more individualistic era, some idea of the "townscape" that a collection of these dwellings created may still be glimpsed along Silay's main thoroughfare today. Despite their many differences, such houses belong to a broad Classical heritage that includes examples as lavish as Juan Nakpil's **Simplicio Lizares Mansion** and the famous **"Ruins"**, both in Talisay . Within this stylistic canon, the Philippine mansions subscribe to the less-doctrinaire

approach of Spanish Classical models – as we shall see in the final, "Local Vernacular" section of this essay.

These Georgian-era examples presage the age of imperial international commerce in new commodities such as oil and cotton. Eve Blau's recent architectural portrait of the "shock" city of Baku in Azerbaijan details how

[its] oil barons competed with one another in the construction of spectacular and bombastic palaces. Architects from Germany, Russia, and Poland were commissioned to design urban mansions in highly eclectic iterations of the Gothic and other revival styles popular in Europe during the 1860s and 1870s, as well as in more eccentric formal vocabularies
- Eve Blau, *Baku – Oil and Urbanism,* Zurich: Park Books, 2018, p. 78

The British city at the receiving end of the booming cotton trade was Manchester, presiding over the widespread network of Lancashire weaving mills. It shared its pattern of textile barons and their lavish suburban mansions with another cotton city – the Gujarati metropolis of Ahmedabad (nicknamed the "Manchester of India") at the other end of the trade. However, while the merchant villas of Manchester's southern suburbs are the epitome of Victorian and Edwardian splendour, those of Ahmedabad's latter-day Medicis bear the unmistakable imprint of 20th-century Modernism. For this was the city that benefited perhaps the most from the involvement of Le Corbusier in independent India.

Contracted to design Chandigarh, the twin-capital of the new Punjab and Haryana states on the northern Indo-Gangetic Plain, the world-renowned French-Swiss architect was also favoured by the shrewd mercantile class of the western city of Ahmedabad, who commissioned some of his most outstanding later works. The resulting Shodan and Sarabhai villas are perhaps the "commodity houses" with the most impeccable Modernist pedigree anywhere.

The Philippine mansions sit somewhere between the "achingly modern" and the "spectacular and bombastic". Not for them the wilder architectural fantasies of Baku's Paris of the Caspian – with a few exceptions such as the extravagant interior of Iloilo's **Celso Ledesma House**. But equally not the blunt directness of Palladio's villas, with which we opened this overview, even the grandest of whose Venetian patrons still expected to store their produce in the attic.[7]

In architecture, sharp edges, points and grey render were proclaimed as symbols of the defeated Germanism while bright colours and roundness were attributed to the victorious Slavs. Cubism was over, and a colourful "National Style" appeared that was later sometimes called "Rondocubism".

Jaroslava Staňková, *Prague: Eleven Centuries of Architecture*, Prague: PAV Publisher, 1992, p. 288

Towards a National Style

In architectural terms, emerging nations have generally faced the question of a new "national" style, and the dilemma of whether or not to borrow aspects from their colonial past – although not many seem to have opted for such an eclectic "free-for-all" as our Philippines examples. The route to a national style has broadly followed one of four avenues.

Starting from Scratch
The deliberate attempt to create a national style *ex nihilo* would pose extraordinary challenges in a cultural milieu as diverse as that of the Philippines, and not even residences with a close political connection to the founding of the Philippine Commonwealth (1935–46) – such as the **Yusay-Consing Ancestral House** – have attempted it. However, it has been seen in more homogeneous Western contexts. Perhaps the starkest example – and a true architectural oddity – is provided by the nascent Czechoslovak state, emerging from the First World War and earlier dominance by Austria–Hungary. The resulting, somewhat forced "National Style" (also referred to as Rondo-cubism) comprised a strikingly eccentric mixture of Cubist forms and patterns/colouring allegedly drawn from ancient Slavic myth. Initially applied to public edifices, Rondo-cubism found perhaps its most satisfactory home in a cluster of unique villas designed by Josef Chochol at the foot of the ancient Vyšehrad fortress in Prague. Ultimately, however, this self-proclaimed "National Style" proved to be an architectural dead end.

A more successful, synthetic central European style can be seen roughly half a century later in neighbouring Hungary, as it emerged from Soviet rule. Here, the architect Imre Makovecz cultivated a much-copied "mythology" referencing, in more ambitious cases, the supposed primitive tent dwelling of the original Magyar steppe dwellers: the *yurta*. This semi-mythical form found its way into the designs of churches, community buildings and the dwellings of Hungary's new rising wealthy class in the Buda Hills overlooking the capital, Budapest.

The debt owed by the Philippine mansions to genuine, rather than semi-mythical, traditional forms is obvious, and forms an important part of their architectural impact, as will be shown in the following, "Local Vernacular" section.

Another form of this approach can be seen in the cautionary tale of Egyptian visionary Hassan Fathy. The conventionally trained young architect underwent a Damascene conversion after travelling through Egypt's Nubian south, coming away with the conviction that Nubian mud construction – "which radiate[d] beauty and culture from every brick and decorative detail"[8] – offered the best possible future for non-metropolitan Egyptian architecture. His subsequent proselytising for this borrowed national style (most Egyptians were ignorant of this southern portion of their country to the extent that his efforts would have constituted "starting from scratch" for them) led to brave attempts at both Gourna, on Luxor's west bank, and New Baris in the country's Western Desert. These employed traditional construction methods directly in a literally "back to basics" model, rather than filtering them through later technological developments as the Philippine houses do (there is, however, a hint of Fathy's rough-hewn approach in the primitivist Chapel of the Cartwheels in the grounds of the **Gaston Ancestral House**).

At Gourna (1945–47), however, Fathy faced hostility from the prospective villagers. Of the many prejudices voiced by these former cliff-dwellers of Luxor's Western Hills, the most striking is that for them the domes that distinguished many of his Nubian-style buildings marked them out as tombs – i.e. houses of the dead.[9] This class-based resistance brings to mind Nobuyuki Ogura, David Yap and Kenichi Tanoue's comments about Filipino Modernist Francisco Mañosa's attempted promotion of plyboo (a plywood-like material formed from folded bamboo sticks), which was spurned by the "people of the wealthy class".[10]

However, as we will see later in the "Local Vernacular" section, it is difficult to imagine Gourna-style hostility to a vernacular idiom in an environment as diverse as that of the Philippines. Such a stark architectural disjunction is perhaps only possible in a nation as rigidly delineated as Egypt – whose settlements have since ancient times hugged the banks of the Nile, and which has long disparaged its own outer fringes.[11]

Finally, it can, of course, be argued that in many ways the Western architectural modes bestowed upon nations such as Egypt during their colonial periods constituted the true "starting from scratch", when often unsuitable forms and techniques were imposed on indigenous societies that had been coping well without them for (in some cases) millennia.

Clockwise from left: **Imre Makovecz building**, Budapest, Hungary (1996); **Hassan Fathy's Nubian vernacular**, Egypt (1940s); **Balay Ni Tana Dicang**, Talisay: *calado*s (transoms); **Chapel of the Cartwheels** (1960s) in the grounds of the **Gaston Ancestral House**, Manapla.

Adopting Existing Styles

A more common path to a national style lies in adopting and/or continuing existing models prevailing inside or outside the country in question. However, despite the conventional nature of this adoptive approach, it can lead to some decidedly unconventional outcomes. The eastern African city of Asmara in what is now Eritrea found itself co-opted by an Italy led by Mussolini at the beginning of his colonial efforts in the region. In the process, young idealistic architects bequeathed Asmara a now world-renowned legacy of modern, and distinctly Italian, monuments – including rare built examples of the peripheral, and otherwise largely theoretical, Futurist style. In a final, unconventional twist, following its integration into and subsequent split from Ethiopia, the young nation of Eritrea now proudly presents the work of Asmara's Italian architects to the outside world as a symbol of its own distinctive national identity.

Something similar but not so extreme happened with another idiom once regarded as peripheral to the mainstream of architectural history: Art Deco. In its heyday, Bombay (now Mumbai), another "cottonopolis" of British India alongside Ahmedabad, pioneered a noted adapted *regional* style – what became known as Bombay Gothic.[12] This pre-Palladian medieval Venetian style, with its breezy colonnades, was as well suited to the shores of the Arabian Sea as it had been to the humid Veneto – similarly to the elaborate but climatically practical *calado* (transoms) of Philippine mansions such as **Balay Ni Tana Dicang** in Talisay and **Nelly Garden** in Jaro, Iloilo. However, in colonial Bombay, expediency saw it give way to a regional variant of Deco, whose stuccoed façades proved less costly than elaborate medieval-style arcades and tracery.

Taken up enthusiastically in the United States, Art Deco (or "Moderne" as it was sometimes called) was also popular in the Philippines, with the once-fashionable thoroughfare of Vito Cruz Street in Manila showing several examples. Filipino architect and writer Augusto Villalón even credits it with presiding over "the change in our … lifestyle … from Fil-Hispanic to Fil-American"[13] – thus raising it tantalisingly close to the "national style" category, and helping to bridge (albeit belatedly) from one colonial era to another. The Philippine sugar mansions also adopted Art Deco – seen most strikingly in the bold massing and nautical lines of the **Lopez Boat House** and the dazzling surface treatments of the **Generoso M Villanueva Mansion** – and, at least internally, in the **Simplicio Lizares Mansion**, some of whose colour schemes recall the bold tones of those Deco exemplars: Napier, New Zealand and Florida's Miami Beach.

Clockwise from left: **Generoso M Villanueva Mansion**, Bacolod (1930s); Leandro V Locsin, **Cultural Center of the Philippines**, Manila (1969); the roofscapes of **Casa Mariquit** (1803 onwards), Jaro; Sedad Hakki Eldem, **Social Security Agency Complex**, Istanbul, Turkey (1962–64).

Given its internationalist credentials, it is not surprising that mainstream Modernism exerted a strong influence on some emerging national styles. The most direct example of this is provided by independent India. In contrast to other nations (the Philippines among them) where the Modernist Master Le Corbusier was admired, the fledgling Indian republic – as we have seen – went one step further and directly engaged him to design what is generally seen as its first new city: Chandigarh. In addition, US/Estonian architect Louis Kahn was invited to contribute the first of independent India's prestigious Institutes of Management. His designs included well-appointed houses for faculty academics in a composition of typically iconic, almost timeless brickwork blocks that shelter each other from the fierce heat and carefully filter sunlight into their interiors.

The presence in the subcontinent of these two "giants" galvanised an Indian architectural scene that would go on to boast the works of Charles Correa and Balkrishna Doshi (both RIBA Gold Medal winners).[14] One of Correa's best-known residential designs – his House at Koramangala (Bengaluru), 1985–9 – even served for many years as then-Bangalore's branch of the pioneering ethical-garment store Fabindia, in an echo of the commercial use successfully found for the restored **Yusay-Consing Ancestral House** in Molo, Iloilo.

Proximity, however, was no dealbreaker: the patron and designer of the **Generoso M Villanueva Mansion** in Bacolod, for example, allegedly never travelled outside their native Philippines. Yet their design exhibits strong traces of a varied early Modernism beneath its Art Deco veneer. Beyond its extravagant terrazzo flooring and ocean-liner touches, this dwelling's tight, curved staircase wall brings to mind the taut lines of the ramp at Le Corbusier's Villa La Roche in Paris or even the playful curves and porthole windows of early-period Hans Scharoun. The latter would go on to become Germany's leading organic architect after the Second World War, but his early Modernist buildings – such as the "gateway" villa to Stuttgart's world-famous Weissenhof Siedlung of 1927 and the curving, swooping Wohnheim in German Breslau (now the western Polish city of Wrocław) from 1929 – already show highly orchestrated and inflected forms pushing beyond Modernism's often dour functionalist envelope.

Adapting Existing Idioms

An alternative approach is to forge a new national style by adapting rather than adopting existing national idioms. This can be seen in the work of the Turkish architect Sedad Hakki Eldem, whose use of Ottoman-style pavilions with vertically proportioned fenestration is most famously to be found in the Aga Khan Award-winning Social Security Complex on Istanbul's Atatürk Boulevard (originally planned to accommodate a medical centre, offices, bank and cafeteria, this is a community building that nonetheless takes great pains to adhere to a domestic scale), and in the sweeping roofscapes of Cambodia's Vann Molyvann and his "New Khmer" style – modelled on, but not enslaved to, traditional Khmer and Thai architecture. Molyvann's own house, of 1970, in Phnom Penh displays a similar kind of oversailing roof to that of Iloilo's **Balay Remedios**, but with more pronounced structural daring.

Such sculptural efforts have also proved popular in a Latin context, and are exemplified by the adventurous vaults and spans of Mexico's Félix Candela. These, tellingly, are attributed not to traditional Aztec architecture but to Candela's educational experience in Spain, where he witnessed the erection of structures by Madrid-based concrete-shell virtuoso Eduardo Torroja. Veteran architectural historian Kenneth Frampton even reminds us that the distinguished Mexican writer Carlos Fuentes "regard[ed] Candela's [dramatic, sculptural] work as a continuation of the Ibero-American Baroque tradition ..."[15]

With this "double Latin" connection in mind, it should not be forgotten that, as Augusto Villalón informs us, "because the Philippines was so distant from Spain, it was administered through Mexico rather than directly from the Iberian Peninsula. Therefore, the Spanish influence in the Philippines carries a heavy Mexican overlay".[16] Certainly, the imposing sculptural forms of Candela and Enrique del Moral find an echo in the monumental work of the late Filipino architect Leandro V Locsin, but are perhaps too emphatic for the subtler Philippine domestic context – as we see in the houses in this book, more often Neoclassical than Baroque (of whatever variant). More striking, perhaps, is the fact that the *palapa* thatched roof form encountered in coastal and desert areas of Mexico is actually derived from a Philippine lean-to construction method (known as *pala pala* – "prop").[17]

Borrowing from Colonial Styles

Our final approach to a national style is perhaps the most common – that of borrowing from general, prevailing colonial (rather than Modernist) models. While countries such as India and Brazil largely eschewed this approach, it can be seen clearly embraced in the Philippines. Here, the aforementioned Spanish/Mexican heritage shines

through and contributes to the diversity and virtuosity of these houses within (with a few notable exceptions) an overarching Classical Revival style.

However, this leads not to slavish imitation as, in contrast to the strict formalising of Palladian Classicism (seen in the previous section), the Iberian approach to this and indeed other prevailing architectural models has always seemed somewhat relaxed. Africa-born architectural critic Peter Buchanan[18] commented that "Spanish architecture has always been very eclectic, drawing on many styles and mixing them freely". Buchanan mused further, in a comment that will apply even more strongly to the Philippines, given Villalón's Mexican reminder above:

Perhaps the Spanish did not apply a style correctly because they were too far in space and time from the sources of each style to really believe in them. Instead of following the rules of a style, they seem to have trusted instinct and been more concerned with space and ambience – very Modernist concerns.
- Peter Buchanan, "Poetics of Modernism: Spain", *Architectural Review* Vol. CLXXIX No. 1071 (May 1986), p. 23

This cheerful unwillingness to apply style "correctly" can be seen in the Mannerist interiors of the otherwise Neoclassical **Celso Ledesma House**, the purported "Antillan" style of the **Gaston Ancestral House** and the loosely Beaux-Arts style of the **Simplicio Lizares Mansion**, which augmented this local idiom with a dramatic, externally expressed staircase and high-level pergola in a manner reminiscent of Prussian master Karl Friedrich Schinkel. As if to prove this point, the intricate façade-screen arrangements of many "Antillan" Philippine mansions (adopted in response to climatic conditions) show a debt to the traditional Japanese vernacular in addition to this Central American/Caribbean-derived style.

With such expansive eclecticism in mind, there is one other notable non-Western parallel with the Philippine mansions in the field of "free-for-all" borrowing of colonial styles. This is the remarkable early 20th-century Garden City district of Cairo, a private development "intended as a wealthy enclave with lush tree-lined streets and an urban pattern that separates it from its surroundings".[19] Here, however, a slight national neurosis rather than confident inventiveness plays a prominent part. At Garden City, it is claimed, aspirational Egyptian designers and patrons favoured any architectural style for their new villas provided

Tropical rainforest climates have no pronounced summer or winter; it is typically hot and wet throughout the year and rainfall is both heavy and frequent.

The Köppen Climate Classification subtype for this climate is 'Af'. (Tropical Rainforest Climate). Köppen-Geiger classification for the Philippines: https://www.weatherbase.com/weather/weather-summary.

it wasn't British or French, representing the country's two previous colonial occupiers.[20] As a result of this act of architectural defiance, here, sandwiched between Kasr el Aini Street and the Nile Corniche, 1920s US-style Art Deco apartment blocks rub shoulders with central European Classical villas and Turkish Ottoman-style mansions. However, despite the architectural ingenuity on display in this slice of Downtown Cairo, in its wholesale stylistic borrowing we are a long way from Buchanan's "eclectic" mixing and "trusted instinct" as witnessed in the Philippines.

Philippine "eclectic" architectural mixing also recalls Vincent Scully's description of early American attempts at grand domestic architecture, and perhaps draws in the cultural influence of the United States.

Any kind of prototype might be employed in the making of such forms: Italian villas, Gothic cottages, and so on … They might be "Tuscan" or "Italian villa," … or "Moorish" … but in essence they are all of the same style: that of free fancy dramatized, at once optical and allusive, hence doubly picturesque.
- Vincent Scully, *American Architecture and Urbanism,* new revised edition, New York: Henry Holt and Company, 1988 [1969], p. 88

Perhaps the Spanish "trusted instinct" and "concern … with space and ambience", cited above, have found a home within American-style examples in the Philippines. After all, the US idiom most often cited with regard to the Philippines is that of a heavy Beaux-Arts approach, associated with government and military buildings, but the Iloilo, Negros and Pampanga houses instead point towards a more flexible tradition – one exemplified by the Californian maverick Bernard Maybeck.[21] His famous First Church of Christ Scientist (1910) in Berkeley has been described as "combin[ing] California carpenter craftsmanship with Byzantine, Romanesque and Gothic Revival influences"[22] and his 1915 Palace of the Fine Arts for the Panama–Pacific Exposition in San Francisco evokes theatrical and Baroque set pieces – a suitable precedent, perhaps, for the confident blending of styles noted in the Philippine mansions.

The Local Vernacular

Despite its being rooted in the certainties of local climate, most authoritatively documented in the Köppen-Geiger system cited above, the traditional vernacular can be a fickle guide. No traces remain in its later merchant *palazzos* of the surprisingly humble original dwellings of Milan: long, low houses that can still be found in places hugging the Italian city's network of narrow canals. In Japan, by contrast, the "Classical" *shinden* style of timber mansion in its own grounds (in a way, the closest thing that the early medieval Heian Period had to Palladianism) persisted for local landlords and merchants up until the Meiji Restoration of 1868.

Nonetheless, it is the rare architectural culture that does not yearn in some way for its version of what Marc-Antoine Laugier saw fit to term the "Primitive Hut"[23] – whether this be the northern pitch-roofed prototype of the Classical Greek villa or temple, the fanciful *cottage orné* of the 18th- and 19th-century Picturesque or even the iconic *etxea* house-barn so essential to the Basque nation and its idea of itself.[24] And in the Philippines, despite the aversion to a strict national style noted above, the rural vernacular prototype of the *bahay kubo* – the island's lowland "square house" – informs many of even the grandest mansions. Certainly, it is impossible to read a monograph on historical Philippine architecture without coming across frequent mention of it, and it is perhaps this remarkably persistent archetype that grounds Philippine architecture and gives it the confidence to embrace the layering of subsequent styles encountered so often in these houses.

The humble *bahay kubo*, the traditional timber-and-thatch house on stilts, shared across much of Southeast Asia, was originally a temporary structure appropriate to the slash-and-burn agriculture practised in the Philippines. Despite its suitability to the prevailing humid and earthquake-prone climate, it transitioned to the more permanent, stone-built *bahay na bato* with the arrival of more settled wet-rice cultivation and the incoming Spanish, determined to replicate the masonry traditions of their homeland.

Nonetheless, this was no one-way process. It underwent a series of iterative "loops" as regular earthquakes highlighted the dangers in the Philippines of taking masonry up to second-storey eaves level and cladding roofs

Clockwise from left: **Bahay kubo**-style hut; **Pison Ancestral House**, Molo, Iloilo (1907); **stone-based bahay na bato**; Intramuros, Manila; **sliding-screen architecture**, Kamakura, Japan.

in the particularly unstable traditional curved tiles. After one especially disastrous earthquake, new building regulations favoured a return to more flexible timber for upper storeys and the introduction of wooden pillars (known as *haligi*) for the lower structure, reducing the masonry to a cladding role. In many instances, corrugated iron prevailed on Philippine roofscapes over the more stable (but costly) European-style flat tiles and the traditional but highly flammable *nipa* (mangrove) palm. The loop back to timber led, among other things, to the remarkable layered, sliding upper façades of Philippine residences, more reminiscent of Japanese *shoji* screens than Iberian or Caribbean solutions (and giving the lie to claims on the Philippine vernacular by unhelpfully cited "Antillan" models). It also led to the development of the "flying" *galleria volada*, the projecting timber storey that wrapped around the upper-level rooms, with its accompanying jalousies, canopies and *calado* – the remarkable pierced transoms that became such a boon to through ventilation and the decorative lexicon alike, as can be seen most demonstratively in the **Jalandoni-Lopez Vito House** in Jaro.

All these features are apparent in the grand houses of the Philippines – along with the distinctive use of *capiz*, a translucent shell, in windows and screens where it proved

safer under earthquake conditions than glass. Another feature stemming from earlier disasters (the islands suffered severe quakes throughout the 1600s) was the use of stone for staircases only up to the first landing. The freestanding staircase, rather than one tucked away and enclosed, had initially been a Spanish innovation; Zialcita and Tinio inform us:

In medieval Europe, the stairway had been a continuous flight of steps that hid in a concealed passageway. The Spaniards exposed the stairway in a great hall and made it mount up, halt at a landing, double turn and mount up imperiously to the upper halls. This made the parade of guests in their lace ruffs and swords, their flowing capes and coats of China silk more spectacular.
- Fernando Zialcita, "A Growing Environmental Awareness", in Fernando N Zialcita and Martin I Tinio Jr, *Philippine Ancestral Houses (1810–1930)*, Quezon: GCF Books, 1980 [7th printing, 2006], pp. 27–28

This performative aspect is particularly apparent at the Jaro mansion known as **Nelly Garden**, about which Villalón asserts, "Its grand staircase incorporates a wide landing at mid-level, called palco (Spanish presidential theatre box) by the owners, where guests of honor sat to watch the dancing and festivities taking place in the immense living room below."[25]

Nonetheless – as Peter Buchanan hints at (in the previous "National Style" section), in the context of Spanish architectural culture – none of this traditional knowledge need preclude "Modernist concerns", and the Philippine mansions should not be excluded from architectural appraisals for being "traditional" or for their debt to the local vernacular. For example, the internal flexibility that sliding screens and walls bring to these tropical houses in the name of ventilation has an echo in the pioneering models of Modernists such as Gerrit Rietveld, whose 1924 Schroeder-Schräder House in the Dutch city of Utrecht took the open plan to then unheard-of lengths. The **Hofileña Ancestral House** even boasted a removable wall to allow its ground-floor living areas to double as a performance space. It can, of course, be argued that the pre-modern Japanese stole a march on all such examples with their full-blown approach to sliding translucent (*shoji*) and opaque (*fusuma*) screens – seen perhaps to best effect in the remarkable 17th-century Katsura Rikyu "Imperial Villa" on the outskirts of Kyoto – lauded in the 1940s by European Modernists such as Bruno Taut.

Finally, the all-encompassing roof, of a kind inherent to the *bahay na bato* (as well as the Basque *etxea*, mentioned above), has been recognised by no less a commentator than Kenneth Frampton. In a 2005 reappraisal of his influential Critical Regionalism concept, Frampton remarked on the prevalence of both "roofwork and earthwork" in the kinds of regionally inflected architecture that he favoured, including the work of many sensitive, "organic" practitioners such as Finland's Alvar Aalto and the Danish Jørn Utzon.

It might be that there is also something in the expressive, sheltering canopies of the sugar mansions of Iloilo, Negros Occidental and Pampanga that helps to successfully gather so many styles and idioms together in a generous, undogmatic and wonderfully inclusive way. Perhaps in this way, the local-vernacular aspect of these mansions "wins out" over trade-based or national-style concerns. It is to be hoped that the preceding chapters have demonstrated the accuracy of this sentiment.

Picture Credits

All images in this essay by Siobhán Doran, except the following, by Ian McDonald: Lübeck, Lavenham, Imre Makovecz (Budapest), Hassan Fathy (Gourna, Luxor), Sedad Hakki Eldem (Istanbul), Intramuros, Kamakura.

Notes

[1] James S Ackerman, "The *Magnificenza* of Palladio's Late Works and Its Legacy Abroad", in Ackerman, *Origins Invention, Revision*, New Haven, CT and London: Yale University Press, 2016, p. 123.

[2] Victor Purcell, *South and East Asia since 1800*, London: Syndics of the Cambridge University Press, 1965, p. 14.

[3] The openness of these former colonies to the work of Team X members Georges Candilis and Shadrach Woods, and Amancio Guedes, respectively, contributes to the diversity observed in those young African states' "national" architectures. It also echoes on a smaller scale the influential presence of earlier Modernist heavyweights such as Antonin Raymond, Le Corbusier and Louis Kahn in independent India (see the following "National Style" section).

[4] Monina Allarey Mercado (ed.), *Victorias: A History in Pictures*, Metro Manila: Victorias Milling Co, Inc., 1989, p. 88.

[5] "The buildings of any period reflect the structure and development of society as much as they do the aesthetics and technology of the time". From publisher's blurb to Bill Risebero, *The Story of Western Architecture*, New York: Charles Scribner's Sons, 1979.

[6] With its imported Belgian brickwork, Port Sunlight – although intended for the workers in Lever's chosen commodity: soap and related products – is surely the most lavish of Britain's garden cities, constructed along with several others loosely after the principles of social reformer Ebenezer Howard.

[7] The topmost storeys of Palladio's mansions required windows set at floor level in order to facilitate ventilation for loose-stored grain, and bands of smooth plaster up to a prescribed height and around doors to deny footholds to "[m]ice that had climbed up this far, attracted by the scent of the grain and beans". Antonio Foscari, *Living with Palladio in the Sixteenth Century*, Zurich: Lars Müller Publishers, 2020, p. 16.

[8] Hassan Fathy, "Inspired by Nubia"; originally published in Arabic: issue 66 of *Al-Majalla*, Cairo, July 1962.

[9] One bizarre result of this situation is that while New Gourna itself lies largely incomplete and neglected, further along the Al Qarna Road in the direction of the Theban Hills, foreign archaeologists and other Western professionals reside in relative luxury under derivative but impeccably maintained Fathy-*style* domes. Regarding the contrast between Fathy's many elite clients and his desire to work for the impoverished *fellahin* of Egypt, Leïla el-Wakil comments, "While the poor were too superstitious to imagine living under a dome, which for them evoked the world of the dead, the wealthy turned their domed *qa'a* [central reception hall] into music rooms. While the disinherited and the populists protested

that 'mud' took its inhabitants back to the Middle Ages, the intelligentsia took residence in cool houses with thick walls made of mud brick or Muqattam stone". Leïla el-Wakil, "The *Qa'a* and the Arab House" in el-Wakil (ed.), *Hassan Fathy Dans son Temps*, Gollion: Infolio éditions, 2013, p. 79.

[10] Nobuyuki Ogura, David Leonides T Yap and Kenichi Tanoue, "Modern Architecture in the Philippines and the Quest for Filipino Style", *Journal of Asian Architecture and Building Engineering* Vol. 1, No. 2 (November 2020), p. 236.

[11] "The Redland was the complete opposite of Egypt, which was characterised as the Blackland … Everything lying outside the Blackland (being defined as the zone of arable land on both sides of the Nile) was considered to be a part of the Redland. Egypt was therefore surrounded by the Redland, which constituted a continuous threat to her stability." Filip Taterka, "The Meaning of the njwt-Hieroglyph: Towards a Definition of a City in Ancient Egypt", in Łukasz Miszk and Maciej Wacławik (eds), *The Land of Fertility II: The Southeast Mediterranean from the Bronze Age to the Muslim Conquest*, Newcastle upon Tyne: Cambridge Scholars Publishing, 2017, p. 27.

[12] Enthusiasm for pre-Palladian Venetian Gothic grew in Britain following the 1850s publication of John Ruskin's *Stones of Venice*.

[13] Augusto F Villalón, *Lugar: Essays on Philippine Heritage and Architecture*, Makati: Bookmark, Inc., 2001, p. 21.

[14] Doshi defined Le Corbusier as "the acrobat" and Kahn "the yogi". Sandro Rolla, architect, Milan; personal communication with the author.

[15] Kenneth Frampton, *Modern Architecture: A Critical History*, fifth edition, London: Thames & Hudson, 2020, p. 390.

[16] Villalón, *Lugar*, p. 3.

[17] I am indebted to Iloilo-based conservationist Eugene Jamerlan for this observation.

[18] Buchanan, who died on 23 August 2023, was eulogised by the Spanish publication *Arquitectura Viva*, with whom he published many articles, in a poignant obituary: "Buchanan … was born in Malawi in 1942, but after studying in Cape Town he settled in London to make his way as an architect and eventually as a journalist, becoming the soul of *The Architectural Review* in the 1980s. From there he promoted Spanish architecture, acquiring an intimate familiarity with the professional landscape of Madrid and Barcelona". Luis Fernández-Galiano, "Remembering Cohen and Buchanan", AV, 2 September 2023. Available online at https://arquitecturaviva.com/articles/agonico-agosto-recordando-a-cohen-y-buchanan

[19] Mohamed Elshahed, "Garden City", in *Cairo since 1900: An Architectural Guide*, Cairo and New York: American University in Cairo Press, 2019, p. 172.

[20] "As if reflecting Egypt's bias against Britain, Cairo's fashionable community avoided colonial villas, choosing instead a mix of new-classical, Venetian … and Gothic pastiches amidst a festival of art deco". Information sheet, Garden City, Cairo, 2014.

[21] "When he was rediscovered in the 1940s architectural critics often depicted him as a rebel from convention, but in fact Maybeck always spoke with reverence about the Ecole des Beaux-Arts. He had a deep respect for Greek and Romanesque buildings, which he considered the seminal works of architecture…" David P Handlin, *American Architecture*, London: Thames and Hudson, 1985, p. 164.

[22] Mark Swenarton, "The California Connection" in Alan Berman and Ian Latham (eds), *Being Ted Cullinan*, London: Right Angle Publishing, 2020, p. 48.

[23] The 18th-century French Jesuit theorist Marc-Antoine Laugier first published his contention that the ideal architectural form embodies what is natural and intrinsic – encapsulated in the typically Enlightenment-era label "The Primitive Hut" – in the 1750s, in the second edition of his *Essay on Architecture*.

[24] "A central concept in Basque identity is belonging, not only to the Basque people but to a house, known in the Basque language as *etxea* … A house stands for a clan …. Each house has a tomb for the members of the house and an *etxekandere*, a spiritual head of the house, a woman who looks after blessings and prayers for all house members wherever they are, living or dead". Mark Kurlansky, *The Basque History of the World*, London: Jonathan Cape, 1999, p. 6.

[25] Augusto F Villalón, "Peeling Away Layers of Ilonggo Architecture", in A Feleo (ed.), *Iloilo: A Rich and Noble Land*, Metro Manila: Lopez Group Foundation, 2007, p. 105.

GLOSSARY OF TERMS

abanico .... a type of folding fan; used to refer to stair winders (q.v.)

apitong .... a Southeast Asian hardwood

apse .... semicircular or polygonal termination of a chapel/church

bahay kubo .... traditional timber-and-thatch house on stilts

bahay na bato .... literally "stone house": Filipino-style house, derived from the original *bahay kubo*

balayong .... a hard wood native to the Philippines; also known as tindalo (q.v.)

baro't saya .... (female) Philippine national dress

barrigon windows .... windows with bulging, "pot-bellied" grilles

bodega .... storeroom

caida .... anteroom

calados .... pierced transoms to provide through ventilation

calesa .... horse-drawn carriage

capiz .... translucent marine shell used for windows and lampshades

carabao .... domestic swamp-type water buffalo native to the Philippines

carroza .... horse-drawn carriage

comedor .... dining room

coquina .... soft, whitish limestone formed of broken shells and corals cemented together

entresuelo .... mezzanine

fusuma .... opaque Japanese sliding screen

haligi .... timber columns for the ground floor of the *bahay na bato* (q.v.)

ilustrado .... the educated, wealthy Philippine intelligentsia during the Spanish era

Lola / Lolo .... Grandmother / Grandfather; can also be Great-Grandmother/-father and Great-Aunt/-Uncle

maestro carpintero ... master craftsman

Mannerism .... a type of late Renaissance architecture that distorted and played with Classical forms and rules

metopes .... square spaces between triglyphs (q.v.) in a Classical temple frieze

minka .... tradition Japanese vernacular house

narra .... Southeast Asian timber primarily used for cabinetwork

nipa .... mangrove palm; used for thatch

padrino .... head of the family

perron .... external stairway to a building

persiana .... louvred windows

porte-cochère .... covered shelter for vehicles at the entrance of a building

rustication .... decorative masonry effect cutting back edges of stones, leaving the central portion rough or projecting

sakada carpinteros ... migrant craftsmen from China

sala (major) .... (main) living room

salomónica .... (Spanish: "Solomon-like") barley-sugar columns

scagliola .... decorative technique in which paint is compounded into the cement of a floor or other surface

shoji .... translucent or transparent Japanese sliding screen

silong .... open ground floor of a traditional house

solihiya .... rattan weaving technique (also known as "caning")

Ta / Tana .... a diminutive for the feminine "Capitana" (leader of a community)

terno .... outfit with matching skirt and top in the same fabric; Philippine gown with butterfly sleeves

tindalo .... a hard wood native to the Philippines; also known as balayong (q.v.)

Tita / Tito .... Aunt / Uncle; can also be extended to cover Great-Aunt/Great-Uncle

triglyphs .... vertically channelled tablets in a Classical temple frieze, representing wooden beam ends in stone

ventanilla .... (Spanish: "little window") small window below the main casement

volada .... enclosed gallery running along the sides of a room

winders .... tapering stair treads

ACKNOWLEDGEMENTS

This book would never have happened without the faith, trust, goodwill and generosity of so many people. We are most grateful to our wonderful sponsors, who never showed any doubt that our project would be completed despite the three-year hiatus caused by the coronavirus lockdown; to our advisors, who pointed us in the right direction, made introductions and accompanied us on our many trips in and around the Philippines; to every house owner and heir – your homes, memories and stories form the essence of this book. And last but not least, we thank our families and friends for their love, loyalty and patience as we leaned on them for support; advice; and, literally, the roofs over our heads as we visited Manila, Iloilo, Negros and Pampanga.

GINA CONSING McADAM & SIOBHÁN DORAN
August 2023

MESSAGE FROM HANS SY

Chairman, Executive Committee, SM Prime Holdings Inc.

SM has been a part of Philippine society from its humble beginnings as a shoe store 65 years ago. As we grew, one of the core values SM has espoused is to ensure that our rich cultural heritage is preserved for future generations in such iconic landmarks as the Molo Mansion, the Iloilo Central Market, Chinabank Binondo and the Jones Bridge in Manila. By preserving and restoring these edifices, we not only honor the past but also provide a visual anchor for the future.

As an advocate of sustainable development and environmental responsibility, we incorporated the use of recycled materials, low-VOC paints, energy efficient lighting and other green features in these iconic landmarks. I hope we inspire others to pursue a respectful approach to stewardship of our cultural heritage while minimizing environmental impact, and to innovate and use sustainable practices for social good.

HOMEOWNERS AND HEIRS

Monsignor GG Gaston ◇ Charet Locsin ◇ Julieta Y Consolacion ◇ Luis Y Consing ◇ Tony & Chona Montinola ◇ Concepcion Ascalon ◇ Rafael & Mariflor Lopez Vito ◇ Rosalinda Piamonte ◇ Vanessa Suatengco ◇ Cedie Lopez-Vargas ◇ Marissa Montelibano ◇ Lourdes Escalante ◇ Jean Jalandoni ◇ Robert Puckett ◇ Rene Hofileña ◇ Rito Peña ◇ Remia Locsin ◇ Marina Go ◇ Elsie & Edgardo Rodriguez ◇ Edwina Ramirez ◇ Evelyn Candelaria ◇ Cynthia Baga ◇ Marco Lazatin ◇ Adjie Lizares ◇ Larry & Bob Lacson ◇ Lilia Villanueva ◇ Chell Jimenez ◇ Luci & Luigi Yunque ◇ Frannie Jison Golez ◇ Reena Gamboa ◇ Tony Villanueva ◇ Cynthia de Leon ◇ Edgardo Pison ◇ Ann Soenen ◇ Mayee & Pablo Fabregas ◇ Kevin Piamonte ◇ Solo & Keeno Locsin ◇ Patrick & Martin Jamora ◇ Amelito Lizares ◇ Risa Sarabia ◇ Jesse Gaston ◇ Jacqueline Candelaria ◇ Marina Yvanovich ◇ Jose Jr & Alberto Concepcion

SPONSORS

SM Prime ◇ Double Dragon Corporation ◇ Union Bank ◇ International Container Terminal Services, Inc. ◇ Aboitiz Group ◇ Ramon S Ang ◇ Celia Peralta Consing ◇ Bong & Maribel Consing ◇ Rafael & Monica Consing ◇ Antonietta Chan ◇ George, Allen, Rusty & Chiqui Ruiz de Luzuriaga

PATRONS

Anthony & Alma Arreglado ◇ Raul & Lucia Consing ◇ Jose Emmanuel & Lea Hilado ◇ Gary P Cheng ◇ Renato & Gloria Peralta ◇ Stefan & Keri Veraguth ◇ Vivian Madrigal

ADVISORS

Rosie Siason Jardeleza ◇ Narzalina Lim ◇ Henry Yusay ◇ Eugene Jamerlan ◇ Maret Follosco-Bautista ◇ Mari Tan Delfin ◇ Lisa Ongpin Periquet ◇ Jocelyn Perez ◇ Richard Tuason-Sanchez Bautista ◇ Monique Consing Cheng

IN GRATITUDE

Hans Sy ◇ Teresita Sy-Coson ◇ Edgar Sia ◇ Enrique Razon, Jr ◇ Edwin Bautista ◇ Justice Diosdado M Peralta ◇ Ambassador & Mrs Teodoro Locsin, Jr ◇ Margarito Teves ◇ Virginia Laurel ◇ Atul, Max & Charlie Chavda ◇ Ken & Harry McAdam ◇ Maria Jones ◇ Mark Priestley ◇ Stuart Finn ◇ Rosalie Treñas ◇ Nieva R Consing ◇ Danby & KriKri Consing ◇ Mae Villanueva ◇ Joey Gaston ◇ Marides Yusay ◇ Mia Cameron ◇ Lourdes L Buenaventura ◇ Mayor Jerry P Treñas ◇ Tim & Ida Siason ◇ Lourdes, Rosalyn, Lulu & Tim Consing ◇ Nena Yaptangco ◇ Ann Divinagracia ◇ Lope & Maricor Consing ◇ Mariquet Renshaw ◇ Victa Magcase ◇ Mel Capistrano ◇ Lalay Suarez ◇ Ricky Gallaga ◇ Ver Pacete ◇ Chita Monfort ◇ Carmela Ledesma ◇ Albert Suarez ◇ Peter Ditching ◇ Lucia Lopez ◇ Dada Trillo ◇ Celine Lopez ◇ Ambeth Ocampo ◇ Maria Ysabel Ongpin ◇ Candy Gourlay ◇ Marijo Consing-Saguigit ◇ Fr Robbie Sian ◇ Ronna Sian Suri ◇ Rica Sian Afable ◇ Bernie & Camille Vergara ◇ Anton Periquet ◇ Jovie & Maryrose Tuazon ◇ Peter Maquera ◇ Joe Chan ◇ Peter Latham-Warde ◇ Rowena Romulo ◇ Chris Joseph ◇ Rolly & Ana Rodriguez ◇ Vit Mawis-Aliston ◇ Louie Torres ◇ Peachy Yusay ◇ Marissa Padilla ◇ Stella Sait ◇ Ellen Samson ◇ Gina Fleming ◇ Gina Williams ◇ Bobby & Rhona Macasaet ◇ Trickie Lopa ◇ Charlene Ching ◇ Evelyn Magat ◇ Mila Guerra Lee ◇ Katrina Hamill ◇ Agnes Tinsay ◇ Ging-Ging La'O Gamboa ◇ Tricia Nichol ◇ Gigi Perrett ◇ Roz Morris ◇ Andrew Merrett ◇ Cristina Juan ◇ Luigi Crespo ◇ Amy Paralisan ◇ Jacqui Bonnin ◇ Aida Mamuad ◇ Rosalie & Kim Talde ◇ Kristine Rojo ◇ Jane Lasangre ◇ Lizette Yulo ◇ Kari Hadjivassiliou ◇ Cyrus & Pervin Todiwala ◇ Grace Fornier Magno ◇ Ann Abello ◇ Janelle Jacinto ◇ Apa Ongpin ◇ Marianna Montelibano Ongpin ◇ Jun Terra ◇ Diane Morris ◇ Craig Scharlin ◇ Chris Hodder ◇ Fe Segundo ◇ Bop Lopez ◇ Anne Marie de la Fuente ◇ Manolet Delfin ◇ Melchor Elisan ◇ Jess Ricalde

With special thanks to Nina Lim-Yuson for her illustrations

CONTRIBUTORS

Gina Consing McAdam

Based in London, Gina Consing McAdam has also lived and worked in Manila, Madrid and New York – and travels often to Paris, where she is a visiting lecturer. She is the author of three books of company and organisational history, including a history of The Lanesborough hotel at Hyde Park Corner, London. Her essays have also been published in noted anthologies of Philippine writing. Gina started her career in communications and marketing at Ace-Compton Advertising & J Walter Thompson in Manila. Today, she is a member of the Institute of Directors, a Fellow of the Institute of Hospitality and a Liveryman of the Worshipful Company of Marketors in the UK. She attended Assumption Convent Herran, St Theresa's College and De La Salle University in Manila, and holds an MA in 20th Century English & American Literature from Newcastle University in the UK. Gina dedicates *Houses that Sugar Built* to her parents.

Ian McDonald

Ian McDonald, a former architect, is a copy-editor and proofreader who works for publishers ranging from the Royal Institute of British Architects to Phaidon, Akkadia Press (a Rizzoli partner), the London Design Museum, the American University in Cairo Press, the Aga Khan Award for Architecture (Geneva), and Zurich-based publishing houses Park Books and Lars Müller. In his architectural career, he worked for Bristol-based heritage/contemporary-design specialists Niall Phillips Architects on art galleries and visitor centres throughout the UK; the long-established (West) Berlin practice of former Team X member Manfred Schiedhelm in the reunified German capital on medium-scale housing projects; and in India – at Shilpa Sindoor Architects in the southern city of Bengaluru and, in Ahmedabad, northwest India, at SANGATH, the office of RIBA Gold Medallist Balkrishna Doshi.

Siobhán Doran

Siobhán Doran is a freelance photographer based in southeast England. She works internationally, capturing architecture and interiors in addition to her own projects, many resulting in exhibitions and publications. These include *The Lanesborough Reimagined* (2015) and *Savoy | The Restoration* (2011). Her work has been shown in the UK and Europe, including at MAST Foundation for Photography in Bologna and London's Royal Academy of Arts. An image from *Houses that Sugar Built* was selected for the 2023 RA Summer Show, and she was named Architecture Photographer of the Year at the Prix de la Photographie, Paris, Exhibition for her "Sala Mayor" series from the same book. Trained in Architectural Technology in her native Ireland, Siobhán worked in building design before undertaking a Photography degree at University of Westminster. She founded her photography practice in 2006.

Paula Hickey

Paula Hickey's graphic design practice, PH Design, specialises in print publishing. She has worked for numerous well-known newspaper and magazine titles in both London and her native Dublin. She has held positions as Art Director on the *Sunday Telegraph Magazine* and (Acting) Art Director/Deputy Art Director on *Cosmopolitan* magazine. Paula has also worked on the launch and redesign of a popular lifestyle magazine in Leeds, the Yorkshire city in which she is based. She has collaborated with Siobhán Doran on a series of photography books and other design projects. Alongside her graphics career she has developed a visual arts practice, completing an MA in 2017 at Leeds Arts University. She has since worked on an environmental, research-led art project with the National Trust and has exhibited her artwork in London, Leeds, Italy and Ireland.

ORO EDITIONS
Publishers of Architecture, Art, and Design
Gordon Goff: Publisher

www.oroeditions.com
info@oroeditions.com
Published by ORO Editions.

AUTHORS
Gina Consing McAdam and Siobhán Doran

PHOTOGRAPHY
© Siobhán Doran

TEXT
© Gina Consing McAdam
© Ian McDonald

TEXT EDIT
Ian McDonald

ILLUSTRATIONS
© Nina Lim-Yuson

BOOK DESIGN
PH Design

PROJECT MANAGER
Siobhán Doran

PRODUCTION MANAGER
Jake Anderson

10 9 8 7 6 5 4 3 2 1 First Edition

ISBN: 978-1-957183-80-0

Color Separations and Printing: ORO Group Inc.
Printed in China

ORO Editions makes a continuous effort to minimize the overall carbon footprint of its publications. As part
of this goal, ORO, in association with Global ReLeaf, arranges to plant trees to replace those used in the manufacturing
of the paper produced for its books. Global ReLeaf is an international campaign run by American Forests, one of the
world's oldest nonprofit conservation organizations. Global ReLeaf is American Forests' education and action program
that helps individuals, organizations, agencies, and corporations improve the local and global environment by
planting and caring for trees